FLOWERS
AFLOAT

An elaborately decorated water can with four castle pictures painted around the lower half as well as a multitude of flowers. It is dated 1903 and is in near perfect condition. Is this typical of work at this period, or did it survive because it was exceptionally good?

FLOWERS
AFLOAT

folk artists of the canals

TONY LEWERY

David & Charles

For Edward Paget-Tomlinson,
historian, artist, friend and mentor.

(Page 3)
A cabin block decorated with a delightful naïve castle picture for a British Waterways boat in the 1950s, possibly by Jack Phillips at the Bull's Bridge boatyard.

A DAVID & CHARLES BOOK

First published in the UK in 1996

Copyright © Tony Lewery 1996

Tony Lewery has asserted his right to be identified as author of this work in accordance with the Copyright, Designs and Patents Act, 1988.

A catalogue record for this book is available from the British Library.

ISBN 0 7153 0145 4

Book design by Diana Knapp
Typeset by ABM Typographics Limited Hull
and printed in Singapore by C S Graphics Pte Ltd
for David & Charles
Brunel House   Newton Abbot   Devon

CONTENTS

INTRODUCTION

This book is a description and history of Britain's finest folk art, one that developed and survived against great odds until the middle of the twentieth century. Its survival at all is surprising in a country that led the world in the process of industrial mass production, but what is even more surprising is that it only has a history of about two hundred years. It was not a continuation of a rural peasant occupation, but a fresh flowering of folk culture on the new transport system that fed the industrial revolution.

The book's main subject is the visual art, the painted canal boats and the people who decorated them, but the art is so intimately involved with the people of the boats that the book also sets out to describe the art in its social context. The paintwork is fascinating and sometimes delightful in itself, but its greater importance is as a symbol of a way of working and living that was sensible from both a human and an environmental point of view. A restatement of some of these values can offer some useful guidance for our own future.

A detail of the involved rose painting technique on T. J.T.'s 1903 can, covering every available space with intricate decoration. There are a few other examples of this painter's work in existence, but there are as yet no clues as to who he was or where he worked.

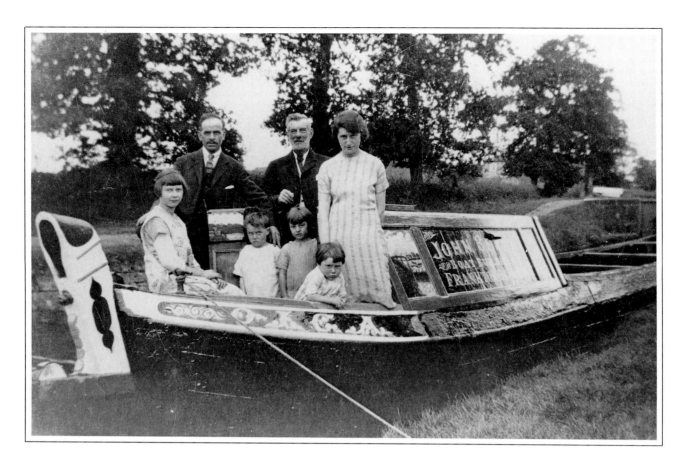

The folk art of the boats was the result of a balanced relationship between the artists who did it, the group that it was done for, and the underlying reasons for its existence. The artists were mainly boatbuilders, craftsmen who decorated the boats in a traditional way as part of their trade, as well as a number of boatmen who became equally skilled in the art; the group was the population of working boatmen, boatwomen and children (and to some degree the carrying companies who employed them), who had been trading on the canals for generations, but the underlying reasons are more difficult to enumerate crisply in a sentence. We have to dip immediately into some difficult concepts – taste and aesthetics, and cultural needs, the very things that define visual art and make it difficult to talk about in words. An outward display of domestic neatness was important, and advertising in a general sense, proclaiming one's taste and prosperity within the boating society; but perhaps above all it was a statement of self esteem, and a mark of membership of an exclusive trade elite.

This traditional art satisfied a cultural need in the boat population for several generations who, because of their insularity and illiteracy, remained largely unaffected by any academic teaching of fine art or the vagaries of fashionable taste. Whilst canal transport in narrow boats continued to support this isolated community, the folk art remained alive and pure, but when commercial cargo carrying finished, the lifeblood was cut off. So many of the inter-related factors changed that what now remains is a rather artificial preserve, a remnant on a life support system. The fact that canal boating is now a hobby, not a working life, has completely changed the equation. What does remain, however, is a mass of

Castle pictures and some very involved lettering on Olga, a change boat belonging to John Beech, boatbuilder and painter, photographed outside his boat dock at Welsh Frankton in 1925. John is standing on the left of the picture alongside his wife Nora and one of his dock workers, Mr Millard.

examples of the old style art, and the memories of many living boat people to be recorded before it is too late.

The painted roses, castles, colours and bright geometric patterns were an integral part of the lifestyle of the narrowboat population of the Midland canals; that lifestyle was the practical way of working and living on the boats, which were in turn the moving parts of the machinery of the canal transport system. Boatmen, boats, architecture and art were all parts of an interdependent combination, a unity of purpose between the trade, the tradesman and the tools of the trade, a rather anachronistic concept in today's commercial world. For a short time in the late eighteenth century, canal building was seen as a practical philosophy – improving the lot of the labouring classes with cheaper coal, food and farm manure, improving the landscape by creating an architectural heritage for the future, whilst simultaneously increasing the canal promoter's own profits

The contrived pile of water cans in this posed photograph at Leighton Buzzard seems to feature several different painters' work. The cabin block underneath the table is especially noteworthy, with its unusual painting of a pair of ploughing horses.

in the present. What a laudable prospect! Perhaps the decoration of the boats was a further extension of this altruistic idealism, for something had encouraged an unnecessary decorative art on some otherwise very utilitarian working craft by the middle of the nineteenth century, when it was first found to be recorded as an existing tradition.

The 'art' on narrow boats ranges across every possible use of the word, from the standard acceptable work of any conscientious craftsman, like the art of the wheelwright, to the fine art of a gallery piece, an item of individual colour and design that has an emotional power quite beyond its original purpose. They were never designed without a practical purpose, of course, and those few painters whose work could be regarded in this light would have been bemused and probably extremely scathing about such an attitude. However, there were a few whose choice of colours, whose layout of the traditional imagery, whose competent handling of the materials, combined with their mood on the day, created objects that express much more than a common piece of painted commercial art should be expected to. These are artists by nature as well as craftsmen by training or practice, those whose inherent artistic talent transforms the standard guaranteed ingredients into something beyond the necessities of the business, the master folk artists in all senses of the words. But even though their work could be shown in isolation in a gallery setting, it would be much less than the whole truth, for it would be ignoring the context for which it was designed, both physical and social, and it would subtract an important layer of its meaning and purpose. The only justification for such an isolated display might be to convince a sceptical viewer that the art of narrow boat painting *can* be viewed in this academic and analytical way, not that it should be. Thereafter that viewer should be drawn back to the canal and the boats, and to the people to whom it belongs.

That, of course, is now virtually impossible. That complete world no longer exists; there is no regular traffic in narrow boats to support the working boat society of which the decorative paintwork was an integral part. There are museums, and there are many enthusiasts, of which I count myself one, desperately trying to record and preserve some of these old canal society values, but we are outsiders looking back. There are also the boat people and their memories, but those with first hand experience of that vanished canal world must necessarily get fewer as the years go by. What does remain is the evidence, and that is what this book seeks to present to the readers for their own interpretation and enjoyment. It is still a work in progress, for many questions remain unanswered, and many canal boat artists remain anonymous, but I hope this book will be accepted as a mark of deep respect towards their memory.

*T*ailpiece *from* The Girls Own Annual, *1882.*

CHAPTER 1

BOATS, BOATMEN AND WIVES 1760–1860

A spritsail barge tied alongside a square-rigged pair of Pickford's narrow boats on the River Thames sometime prior to 1828, when this etching by E. W. Cooke was produced. It offers some interesting early information about the decoration of the top planks, and shows diamonds painted on the top panels of the cabin doors. Compare this drawing with the painting of the Hope, *illustrated opposite.*

Narrow boats did not exist before about 1760. There were all sorts of coastal craft and river barges, built to a wide variety of regional styles and widths; but canal boats built to the narrow 7 feet (2 metres) beam gauge, that became the common denominator of the Midlands canals, were a direct result of the principles and problems of canal building in the eighteenth century. Narrow beam canal boats, approximately 70 feet (21 metres) long by 7 feet (2 metres) wide, had no reason to exist before the Bridgewater Canal was built in 1759, and we can therefore assume that their working population and extraordinary paintwork did not exist either.

Canal boats did not need to be seaworthy in the proper nautical sense as they only operated on calm inland waterways, without waves. They just needed to float. They had to carry the maximum cargo possible to earn their living, but in those early days they also had to be as shallow and narrow as possible to minimize the size and construction costs of the canals built to accommodate them. The first canal boats were all horse drawn, pulled with a long towing line from a mast on the boat by a horse on the towpath alongside the canal, and that horse-power was another factor in the design of the boat. Much of the effort needed to move a loaded barge is in opening an initial passage through the water; having done so it takes relatively little additional power to keep pulling more boat through the hole, an additional practical argument for a long thin carrying craft.

It is probable that the basic design was developed on the Duke of Bridgewater's canal near Manchester, which opened in 1761, where the canal penetrated deep into the mine workings in Worsley Hill. Thin boats could navigate into the very narrow tunnels whilst long boats of a simple box section could carry a lot of coal out. A book published in 1779 quotes an even earlier leaflet about the proposals for the Trent and Mersey canal thus:

> The canal and vessels are to be constructed on the plan found most eligible, from various experiments made on the Duke of Bridgewater's navigation [by] his excellent engineer, Mr Brindley. . . The boats are to be seventy feet in length, six feet wide, to draw near thirty inches water and to carry twenty tons burthen. . . There is to be a man and a boy to each boat, which one horse will draw with ease along the canal . . .
>
> (LOUNDES, 1779)

Detail of a painting by an unknown artist of the Pickford's boat Hope *somewhere on the Oxford Canal about 1820. No fancy painted decoration is visible, but the use of bright bold colours is already quite clear.*

Clearly a gauge of boat had already been determined before the main canals of the Midland network were designed and built in the 1760s and 1770s: the Grand Trunk Canal from the Trent to the Mersey, the Oxford to Birmingham, and the Staffordshire and Worcestershire canals. The locks that pass boats up and down hill ultimately define the maximum dimensions of the boats, and all these early canals had locks roughly 70 feet (21 metres) long by 7 feet (2 metres) wide. A gauge had been set for all the future linking branches, and it remained the most restraining but conserving factor for the following two hundred years.

The expanding canal network of the late eighteenth century was a success and paid many of the early promoters very handsomely, but their success encouraged a number of less well conceived schemes which failed to generate traffic or profit. Gradually it became apparent that canals were not the cast-iron money-making certainty they had seemed to investors at the height of the canal building mania in the 1790s. Consequently, when significant competition was seen to be coming from tramways and the new-fangled steam railways in the 1830s and 1840s, investors lacked the confidence to commit yet more huge sums of money to widen and modernise the narrow gauge canals, to make them more competitive. They were still viable and remained valuable, but they stayed the same size. As the locks remained unchanged so the boats had to remain the same size. The methods of working them continued and the population of working boatmen and women, now a couple of generations old, continued to practise their trade and develop their insular lifestyle. An important part of that lifestyle was already their decorative art.

In 1858 a series of articles called 'On the Canal' appeared in the magazine *Household Words*, describing a journey aboard a canal boat from London to Birmingham. They were written by John Hollingshead in a light hearted style, but with careful observation of detail, and they make fascinating reading for a modern canal enthusiast and historian. He describes the boat and its cabin, and the canal people he meets and travels with; but what is particularly important to this book's interest is his detailed description of the paintwork. He comments on the boatman's taste – 'his rude uncultivated love for the fine arts' – and the brilliantly painted water can 'shipped from a bankside painter's yard at an early period of the journey'. It is the earliest written description of narrow boat art discovered to date, and although as yet unsupported by any corroboration from other sources, his observation of everything else on his journey is so accurate that we may reasonably assume that his description of the paintwork can also be taken as reliable evidence. Several further references will be made to Hollingshead's articles later, but it is the date of publication which is especially noteworthy at this point. Decorative paintwork in a style that had become traditional by the twentieth century was certainly in existence in 1858, and it is described in such a way that it would appear to be not unusual on a canal boat of this period. Where had it sprung from?

In the search for an explanation or possible derivation, a logical if lazy step is to look for a modern parallel, some similarity of colourful expression or imagery, and then to search for possible connections. If one tries hard enough some connections can usually be found, or hints can be elaborated into evidence; the widely held supposition that the boat people were originally of gypsy stock is a good example of this process. The most influential author to succumb to this temptation was L. T. C. Rolt, for it was his book *Narrow Boat*, published in 1944,

which generated a great deal of interest in canals at a very critical time in their history. It led directly to the formation of an organised movement to preserve and restore the canals, which has led by degrees to the huge holiday industry of the present day.

In his book he notes the boat people's 'inborn gypsy love of colour and polished metal', an idea that is fully developed into a racial theory in his second canal book in 1950, *The Inland Waterways of England*. He discusses their surnames, their local characteristics and the similarity of boat cabin to gypsy wagon, although he has to admit that cabins probably preceded the decorated wagons, which only took to the roads in the middle of the nineteenth century and reached their apogee of elaboration in the late Victorian and Edwardian period. Nevertheless their wandering lifestyle and competence with horses gradually convinces him of the gypsy connection, the paintwork being the final proof:

> The nearest equivalent of canal boat decoration is to be found in the carts of the Balkan peasantry which are bright with painted flowers. May it not be that at the time James Brindley cut the Duke's Canal there was encamped on Trafford Moss a tribe of gypsies fresh from the Balkans who had brought with them the first vans, the tradition of painted flowers, and the recollection of the fairytale castles of Eastern Europe which they perpetuated in paint? (ROLT, 1950)

The castle trademark on a Pickford's bill of exchange dated 1815 in Manchester, where they had been operating from Castlefields basin since 1794. Might this printed image have been painted on the boats as well?

It was an appealing notion, and remains so, especially to those of us brought up in the drab days of the 1950s when anything colourful or flamboyant was generally assumed to have a foreign influence. British over-reaction against the decorative excesses of the Victorians, combined with wartime scarcities and post-war austerity had developed a myth of acceptable Britishness – respectable, reserved and dressed in careful grey. Meanwhile, 'folk art' was what Hungarian peasants did, and anything rich and vibrant with colour like the canal boat tradition was almost unconsciously assumed to have a foreign origin, an assumption that Rolt and several others at this period exemplify.

There is, however, no evidence of this ancestry. Another book that will be referred to several times in this chapter is *The Canal Boatmen 1760–1914* by Harry Hanson, published in 1975. This is a thorough scholarly sifting of a mass of evidence from the early days, an invaluable and dispassionate report, and a useful antidote to the more subjective and romantic attitudes of some modern canal enthusiasts, a breed to which this author confesses membership. In his first chapter Hanson considers the boat people's possible gypsy origins very carefully, but cannot find sufficient evidence to suggest that gypsies took to the boating life in any significant numbers.

From the perspective of a couple of centuries it looks as if the canals came into existence very quickly, and one might therefore suppose that there was an immediate shortage of skilled labour to build and work the boats. The temptation is to suppose that this vacuum was immediately filled by one racial or occupational group, one whose traditions would perhaps continue to influence the canal boat population for the next two hundred years. In fact the first narrow canals were being built and opened section by section during the twenty years from 1770 to 1790, with many more links and branches still to be added until 1830, when the canal building age slowed to a halt. There seems little reason to suppose that labour to work the boats was not recruited steadily as the need arose. Navvies from the construction gangs, farm workers who felt they could better

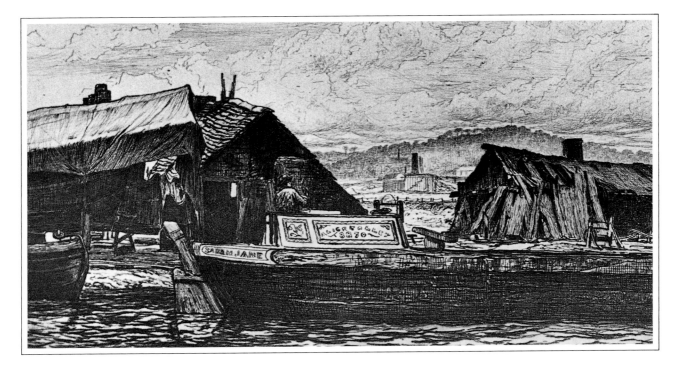

An etching dated 1872 of Monks Wharf, Tipton, the boat dock belonging to Thomas Monk, where he maintained a large fleet of canal boats. According to the fancy name plate on the cabin side, the Sarah Jane belonged to Alice Tolley, and appears to carry some sort of floral design on the stern panel.

their lot with the canal companies, and itinerant labourers from all over the British Isles would be drawn to the new works by the expectation of better wages. Canal boating is difficult to do badly, and any sensible carter in one year could be a competent boat captain by the next.

Hanson suggests very persuasively that a large proportion of the earliest boat crews on the Birmingham Canal in the 1770s had previously been road carriers connected to farming, for farmers with their wagons and horses had traditionally provided a road haulage service to their locality in slack agricultural periods. Some were recorded to be providing the same service to the canal construction industry, and he concludes that there were:

> . . . men of some small local substance who worked in the construction of the canal as carters, and as the water flooded into the completed sections they transferred from carting to boating, and then came to take up this new occupation permanently. Their boat was a floating cart. (HANSON, 1975)

This farming connection provides a possible explanation and origin for some of the designs that occur within the narrow boat painting tradition which seem quite unrelated to any nautical tradition. Carts and wagons were also painted in strong colours, but their main decoration was in the chamfering and carving of the vehicle's framework and undercarriage, nominally to reduce weight without sacrificing strength, but taken to such an elaborate degree that it became an extremely decorative technique in its own right. This process was taken to its most decorative extreme on the living wagons of the gypsies and fairground showmen of the late nineteenth century, but some of these chamfering patterns appear on the boats too, both in physical reality, as on the gracefully shaved edges of the cabin block and gangplank stands, and as two dimensional designs used as painted borders around the cabin hatches.

CANAL SOCIETY

The most significant factor that sets the canal boatman apart from any other contemporary group of workers was the presence of women living and working on the boats, leading to the creation of a complete boating society, cut off and independent of mainstream life on the bank. The point at which they arrived and 'family boating', as it became known, became common, is possibly the key period in the development of the painted tradition. It is usually accepted that because the floral and pictorial boat decoration has a rather pretty and feminine quality it therefore has its origins in the coming of the women to live and work on the boats. This may be so; it is an idea that appeals to the common conception of a female influence; but there is no real evidence for this. In fact some evidence almost suggests the reverse. Hollingshead's trip in 1858 was made aboard a fly boat belonging to a company that only employed all male crews, and whose boats were never allowed to become family boats. The painted decorations were already in place on this boat, however, and apparently had been for some time.

The point at which women were present on the boats in sufficient numbers to be regarded as an important part of the social mix in canal working society is difficult to establish, for much the same reasons that the painting tradition is difficult to pinpoint. At an early period women (and painted flowers) were presumably so rare that they were not worth mentioning; at a later date they had become so common that they were again barely worth mentioning, because the presence of both women and painted decorations on canal boats was such common knowledge. What happened in between seemed unimportant at the time, and remained largely unrecorded. What evidence we have brackets the period somewhere between 1819 and 1858. Hassell's *Tour of the Grand Junction Canal* in 1819 mentions boat crews approaching Blisworth tunnel giving the '. . . steerage to the women, one or two females generally attending each boat', whilst by the time Hollingshead was writing, families on working boats were common, '. . . the pictures of family-barges . . . which pass us at every turn. There is the boatman, and his wife, a stout, sunburnt woman; and children varying in number from two to ten and in ages from three weeks to twelve years'.

The minimum crew necessary for a canal boat was two; one to steer the boat whilst the other drove the horse and prepared the locks. Captains were paid by the trip according to the tonnage carried, but had to pay the wages of crew out of that income, so there was a considerable financial advantage in taking a wife along on the trip and using her as an unpaid crew. In addition, the costs of maintaining a land-based home were also solved if the boat cabin was used as the only family home as well. It is not surprising therefore that family boating should have developed to some degree. Notwithstanding this bleak reasoning, Hanson's detailed analysis suggests that the move to family boating was probably as much social as economic, for the comforts and company of family life as much as for the money. He concludes:

> Boats [of the Canal Age] travelled faster and further, and boatmen were called upon to work more arduously, for which the master boatmen at least were generally well rewarded financially . . . The arrival of wives and families on board slow boats, usually as a substitute for the hired hand[s] meant that the creation of a root-less separate society was assured. This was already distinguishable in the 1830's if it were not yet as isolated as it was to become. *(HANSON, 1975)*

One of only a very few water cans to survive from the nineteenth century, in very good condition and featuring an interesting range of flowers.

Rosie Agnes at Braunston in the late 1930s, a nostalgic glimpse of family boating at its most attractive, tied up with the washing done, with some time to talk to the children. Unfortunately, the best pictures were often taken in the best weather, and they tend to give a rather rosy impression of the hardships of the boating life.

Three related points are important to our researcher in his conclusions: the period, the emergence of a separate society, and their economic standing. Compared with other working classes of the same period, they should be regarded as a tough but respectable segment of society; they maintained a close knit family life and earned enough money to buy more than just the bare necessities of life. There was possibly even enough to pay for extra decoration to their boat homes, certainly more than most of the urban poor could spare to decorate their court and cellar dwellings in the industrial slums. From a twentieth century perspective, the boat population in their tiny cabins may seem like the poorest of the poor, but in the early nineteenth century they were members of and workers in a respectable and prosperous trade. It is therefore in the tastes and aspirations of a better class of labourer and his family that we might expect to find clues to the origins of the decorative arts of the canal boats of the period.

But the boat populations were not popular with settled society any more than the gypsies were. Here today and gone tomorrow, they were the ideal scapegoats for any unsolved mysteries or minor crimes. A dread of their uncivilised behaviour went before them, a reputation that pre-dates the canals and one that lasted until the end of commercial carrying. Many former boating families are still extremely reticent about revealing their past occupation to strangers, because they still fear the effects of their house neighbours' preconceptions about 'dirty bargees', even twenty or thirty years after they left the boats, so strong was the prejudice. It is true it was a tough job, with very long hours, and anyone slowing the progress of the boat with which they were earning their

piece work wage was likely to get the rough end of the tongues of boatmen and women alike. It was also true that they inherited a reputation from the barge-men and bowhauliers of the rivers from the seventeenth and eighteenth centuries, and some canals made detours round private estates, and had the towpath built on the opposite side to the house because the landowners already feared the depredations of the boatmen in advance of their existence. And there was provocation. A slow-moving boat in the middle of the canal was an easy target for mischievous boys and adolescent hooligans with missiles or abuse, and patience was tried beyond limits in every suburb.

In truth the boat population were no better than any other group of indus-trial workers, but they were certainly no worse either. The expectation set up by common prejudice, and the truth as it came to be revealed, has been forcefully documented by Hollingshead:

> . . . [tea] was the favourite and only drink, night and day – except water – not only of our own sturdy boatmen, as far as my observation went. Beer and spirits were lit-tle used, and a pipe being a rare indulgence. Melancholy pictures of drunken brawls, improper language, constant fights, danger to life and property, hordes of licensed ruffians beyond the pale of law and order, which my cheerful friends had drawn the moment they heard of my intention to make an unprotected barge jour-ney, all proved false before the experience of a few hours, and *shamefully false* before the further experience of a few days. We were inmates of a new home and friend of a new family; whose members were honest, industrious, simple and natural.
>
> (HOLLINGSHEAD, 1858)

Perhaps the decorative tradition developed to spite this undeserved reputation, a visual rebuttal of the common expectation.

THE NARROW BOAT CABIN

Hollingshead also offers us the earliest description of the inside of a boat cabin, and in such detail that we can be sure that the standard layout was at least a set convention by the 1850s, if not quite the formal tradition it was to become. He describes it as 'the smallest place of its kind in the whole world', and the nature of the domestic life possible within these tiny spaces must surely have a great deal to do with all the decorative traditions of the people who lived in them. Even after the Canal Boat Act of 1877 these cabins were only officially restrict-ed to being home to no more than two adults and two children under twelve, but many boat cabins continued illicitly to be the home of much bigger families than this well into living memory.

Most house dwellers' bathrooms are far bigger than a traditional narrow boat cabin, and all of them are higher. This tiny living space could not be made any bigger for several reasons which are perhaps worth remembering and repeating before describing the cabin in detail, for it was the physical constraints imposed by cargo carrying that shaped the tradition in the first place. The cabin cannot be wider than the boat for the obvious reason that it couldn't squeeze through the locks, and it cannot be higher than the lowest bridge that it goes under when unloaded, and riding high out of the water. Motor boats can have higher cabins because the weight of the engine and fuel always keeps the stern lower in the water whether loaded or not, but the raised cabin floor over the propeller shaft again reduces the inside headroom to much the same height as a horse boat. The

length of the cabin from front to back cannot be much longer than 10 or 11 feet (3 or 3.5 metres). If it were longer it would decrease the carrying capacity too much for light loads like timber, and the boat would not pay its way; whilst heavy cargo would concentrate too much buoyancy at one end and severely strain the structure of a wooden narrow boat. Some later steel butty boats had extensions built on to their cabins, but the problem was then to stack the cargo high enough at the back end of the hold to push the boat down in the water. The size of the traditional stern cabin is the common denominator between all these physical constraints, made even smaller by tipping the cabin side inwards to avoid the arch of the bridges and tapering the bottom of the boat inwards to make it swim better. Then the family moved in. The fact that sanity was possible in this tiny space, never mind a very rich lifestyle, is due in part to the brilliant organisation of the space by the standard furniture and fittings developed over two hundred years of canal carrying.

Boat cabins are entered from the stern through a pair of narrow doors. The vertical planks of these doors are braced against warping and splitting by two pieces of wood fixed at top and bottom with the grain running across the doors; these strengthening pads have the corners chamfered off all round, and a little recessed and moulded panel is fitted between them. This design has been the standard pattern for narrow boats for years and the topmost panel of each door is the commonest place for a painted castle landscape, with a bunch of roses painted in the recess below.

There is a full length seat-cum-locker built inside the cabin on the starboard

side called the *side-bed*, an important piece of furniture and a vital piece of people engineering. Because it immediately narrows the total floor space by a third, it makes the cabin too small to walk around in, and the occupant is almost forced to sit down and stay still, and take up less space. Part of it may become a child's bed at night, but its main function is as a fixed seat opposite the stove and table-cupboard. Loose boards on the top give access to the storage inside, and a small door in the front near the floor is for a chamber pot, largely superseded in the days of the motor boat by a bucket in the engine room, or perhaps something even more civilised.

The cooking range, now regarded as traditional, is a comparative newcomer, for the normal stove supplied by the carrying company was an open-fronted cast-iron 'bottle' stove. If the crew wanted a range they bought it themselves. It followed that when they changed boats the range went with them and it became a much respected personal status symbol. It suffered the usual frenetic house-proud zeal of the boatwoman and ended up blackleaded and polished to a high shine, or even filed and burnished with emery cloth and wire wool to bare shiny metal. The standard practice is for the range to sit directly on a specially con-structed shelf built just inside the cabin doors on the left, where the rising heat keeps the boat steerer's legs warm. The smoke escapes up the custom made *mid-dle pipe* chimney that is kinked to suit the angle of the cabin side, and then via the *top-pipe* outside, a black removable chimney latterly decorated with polished brass rims and a fancy chain. Coal for the fire is kept in a box that fits snugly into the stern of the boat with the front edge fitted with a 2 inch (5 centimetre) thick ash block to double as a step in and out of the cabin. Needless to say, the side facing into the cabin would be painted with a design, flowers or a castle, and the ash step was scrubbed until it was white.

The length of the cabin is divided into three sections by the frames of its con-struction. The first is a steel strap bracing the cabin planking together without reducing the headroom too much, but the last third is formed by a massive frame of oak stanchions and a curved roof beam; this provides the positioning frame for a vertical bulkhead on the left hand side of the central passageway. Beyond it is built a floor to ceiling cupboard, the central door of which hinges down to make a level bridge with the side bed opposite to create the *cross-bed*. The

This engraving of Susan appeared in the Illustrated London News *to describe the typical canal boats working into London at the time of the disastrous explosion under 'blow-up-bridge' on the Regents Canal in 1874. It appears to be carefully observed, and clearly shows some sort of decorative pictures either side of the name panel on the cabin sides.*

◆◆

(Opposite above)
An attractively decorated tunnel lamp in the Gloucestershire Folk Museum collection, painted with unusually soft, subtle roses.

◆◆

(Opposite)
Sarah Jane and Forget me Not, a pair of horse boats belonging to Henry Grantham, certainly before 1928 when Forget me not was converted to a motor boat.

◆◆

mattress and bedding is now rolled out from the cupboard thus opened and the accommodation is complete. It is a narrow bed for two adults, being rarely more than 3 feet 6 inches (1 metre) wide, but at least it is difficult to fall out of . . . Lucky really, for there were often a couple of infants tucked in as well. The remaining section of cupboard over the foot of the cross-bed, fitted with its own central door, is used for clothes, and the spaces underneath are occupied by the largest possible drawers sliding on runners close to the floor.

Next to the cross-bed cupboard, built astern of the main cabin frame described earlier, is the centrepiece of the cabin, the *table-cupboard*. This is a vertical-fronted cupboard from floor to ceiling halfway along the left-hand side of the cabin, angled slightly to face the cabin doors at the back. The door to the top half is hinged at the base, and swings out and down until its extended inner surface jams under a strong shelf inside the cupboard, to turn the door into a self supporting table extending across the cabin. This table flap is generally rounded at the end to make it more comfortable to get round, and so the cupboard opening has an arched top to suit, a very satisfactory and important element of the architecture of the cabin.

There are a few variations to this shape, like a semi-octagonal top, or a semi-circular shape extending out from a square table. Hollingshead describes his captain's table cupboard as 'gothic arched', but each shape is designed to leave an interesting hole as much as a comfortable table. It was often used as a china cabinet, and with the best pieces on display and each shelf sporting a crocheted hanging lace pelmet, it became very much the central visual focus of the cabin space, like a kitchen mantlepiece in a cottage. The outside of the door has a central recessed panel with wooden moulding in the corners, the most common

Part of a page of illustrations of canal life used on the cover of the Graphic in 1875, and in several subsequent publications. Despite the best efforts of the artist, this cabin still manages to look more spacious than it actually was, for they were no more than 10 feet (3 metres) from front to back and only just over 6 feet (2 metres) wide at the widest part inside the bed, where the mattress is seen rolled up in the left hand drawing. Note the cast-iron 'bottle' stove for heating and cooking, standard canal boat equipment until the 1930s when they were supplanted by small cooking ranges with an oven.

Interior - from Door

Interior from Bed

Canal Boats

place of all for a built-in framed picture of a castle, and the curved section above often has a tiny mirror built into it. Below this cupboard door-cum-table-flap is a cutlery drawer, and below that another, normally opening, cupboard door that gives access to the *boot cupboard*, although in a fine-lined boat it is hardly deep enough to stand a milk bottle in. John Hollingshead talks of 'drawers running down to the floor' beneath his table, but this was certainly uncommon more recently, and a single cutlery drawer became standard.

The main cabin frame that divides the bed space from the rest of the cabin often has the addition of some curved facing pieces in the top corners to create a more attractive archway effect. Although just cut out of a bit of planking and nailed on to the face of the beam, these curved decorative brackets echo the shape of the grown knees of wooden ship construction, and may perhaps be the final remnant of ancient shipbuilding practice, cheapened and lightened during the course of canal history. On the right-hand side the cabin frame some-times supports a very narrow bulkhead curving down from the roof to the top of the side-bed, but it is rarely more than a single plank wide or it would sub-divide the length of the side-bed so that nobody over five feet long could ever lay down on it. However, the Canal Boats Act 1877 states that in boats built prior to 1878 'the part of the cabin which may be used as a sleeping place by the husband and wife shall at all times while in actual use be effectively separated from the part used as a sleeping place by the other [adult] occupant of the cabin by means of a sliding or otherwise moveable screen or partition of wood or other solid mate-rial, so constructed or placed as to provide for efficient ventilation'. The comi-cal remnant of the boatbuilders' answer to this requirement is the 'modesty flap', a little door hinged on to this narrow bulkhead to swing across and subdivide the cross-bed from the remaining side-bed. It is rarely more than a foot square, and often less, and morality was far more likely to be protected by the heavy lace edged curtains that could be drawn across the opening to the bedspace at night. It does, however, provide the boat painter with yet another recessed panel or surface for castles or roses.

Near the door of Hollingshead's boat cabin was 'a single strap, very small, con-taining papers' nailed to the ceiling, a system that was superseded in later days by the *ticket drawer* installed just inside the doors to the left, in the upper corner between the ceiling and the back of the cabin. This contained all the lock pass-es, loading tickets and registration certificate, convenient to the hand of the boat steerer, for checking by canal company officials. On the right, a plank runs down from the roof to the step to become the side of yet another cupboard over the end of the single bed. The alcove below this cupboard often contains a box with a sloping lid like a tiny writing desk, known as the *blacking box* or *monkey box*. In modern times this alcove became the perfect place for the radio.

The back of the cabin is also built up on massive frames of oak, and beneath the ticket drawer on the left the frame is planked both front and back to enclose the 3 inch (7 centimetre) space between. Two shelves are built into this gap, reached by semi-circular holes cut in the interior panelling, one above the other; the upper, smaller one known as the *soap 'ole*, whilst the lower one is sometimes called the *windlass 'ole*. A similar hole is often made to match in the alcove below the side bed cupboard as well, but this creation of tiny storage spaces between the frames at the back of the cabin does not seem to have hap-pened at the front of the cabin where the construction is similar, although wider.

Interior of the cabin of the horse boat Friendship *now on display at the Boat Museum, Ellesmere Port. Graining and decoration by Herbert Tooley of Banbury dock.*

Perhaps the extra 4 inches (9 centimetres) of elbow and pillow room was too much of a sacrifice on a three-foot wide bed.

The style and architecture of a traditional cabin is heavily influenced by the technique with which the woodwork is finished off. Doors are built wherever possible with a central recessed panel with moulding in the corners; although the intention is presumably to create the impression of high quality furniture, with central panels slotted into a jointed and rebated frame, in fact the effect is created by simply nailing the framing pieces on to the background planking. The technique is crude but cheap, and with the addition of moulding, mitred and nailed into every available corner, the effect is quite rich, especially to modern eyes. Each section of the cabin side has 3- or 4-inch (7- or 9-centimetre) moulded framing fitted round it to make yet more built-in picture frames for the decorator to use, and cabin frames and door pillars will be stop-chamfered neatly, or have a beaded edge planed along them. With every corner of the cabin fitted with panelling and moulding, which could incidentally disguise some fairly rough carpentry, the whole lot was painted and grained to a light oak colour, with the mouldings picked out in contrasting colours to finish it off. In the most elaborately decorated cabin, every panel will then carry a beautifully painted castle picture or a bunch of roses.

A decided drawback to this building technique was one of the perpetual problems of the boat population – bugs. With all these separate pieces of planking drying out and shrinking, particularly in the cosy heat of a box the size of a packing case, warmed by a fire big enough for a house, there were lots of cracks large enough for these flat bodied insects to live in. Once a boat gained a few of these extra inhabitants they were almost impossible to get rid of, regardless of regular

A mass of decoration, and an interesting contrast of female headgear, young and old, aboard the John Griffith's boat Wye. The cabin block on the nearest boat appears to feature a picture of a lighthouse instead of the more usual castle scene.

A cabin box decorated for Isabella Salt, dated 1891 inside the lid. The top carries a castle picture, the ends have groups of flowers on green panels but the front, illustrated here, is decorated with an unusually domestic rural scene.

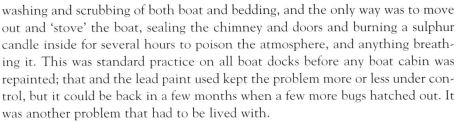

A light-hearted cartoon comment in the Graphic *of 1873, but all the details seem so well observed by the artist that the layout of the castle panel on the cabin side of the* Lovely Polly *narrow boat can probably be believed as well.*

washing and scrubbing of both boat and bedding, and the only way was to move out and 'stove' the boat, sealing the chimney and doors and burning a sulphur candle inside for several hours to poison the atmosphere, and anything breathing it. This was standard practice on all boat docks before any boat cabin was repainted; that and the lead paint used kept the problem more or less under control, but it could be back in a few months when a few more bugs hatched out. It was another problem that had to be lived with.

Apart from the furniture, a number of other items were essential for the comfortable boat cabin life. The drinking water can, kept on the roof next to the chimney, was an official part of the boat's equipment required by the Canal Boat Acts, whilst a *hand bowl*, a tinware washbasin with a handle like a saucepan, usually hung beneath the ticket drawer in front of the soap hole, the bottom of which was another favourite place for more decorative paintwork. A square wooden stool could be useful, especially if the top was hinged and it could double up as a sewing box; and a *seatboard*, a piece of plank to replace the cross-bed during the day, supplied a seat at the table whilst saving space.

It is difficult to know at this distance in time whether the Canal Boat Acts made any difference to cabin construction, or whether they just officially sanctioned what had become normal practice anyhow. Their main criteria for the numbers allowed to occupy a cabin was the cubic capacity of air allowed per person, which worked out on average as two adults and two children in a narrow boat stern cabin. The height in the middle of the cabin was multiplied by the length and the greatest internal width to arrive at a gross capacity from which a certain amount was subtracted depending on the number of built-in permanent cupboards. 60 cubic feet (2 cubic metres) of air was reckoned enough for an adult, and 40 (1.25 cubic metres) for a child, although there is a provision that in boats built prior to the first Act, 30 cubic feet (1 cubic metre) was deemed enough for a child under twelve, suggesting that cabins were expected to be built slightly larger than usual afterwards. Different proportions of air space had to be subtracted for different amounts of furniture, and the figure was slightly less again if the cabin was less than 5 feet (1.5 metres) high! Then these rules of occupation had to be cross-calculated with other rules for separation of the sexes, whereby for example 'a cabin occupied as a sleeping place by a person of the male sex above the age of fourteen shall not at any time be occupied as a sleeping place by a person of the female sex above the age of twelve years, unless she be the wife of the male occupant . . .' but these rules made little difference to cabin design.

REFORM AND THREAT

These Canal Boat Acts of 1877 and 1884 were almost entirely the result of the reforming zeal of one man, George Smith, who had already successfully promoted

*C*abin side castle painting on Charlie *belonging to* Charles Abell of Atherstone, *photographed near Rugby; possibly the work of one of the painters at the two Sephton boatyards near Coventry, about 1927.*

A detailed view of an unusual style of attractive flower painting on the end of an old cabin stool. The painter is unknown, but it is thought he may have worked in the Manchester area.

legislation to outlaw child labour in the brickfield of Leicestershire where he worked. Then he turned his attention to family boating and canal boat children, and launched a virulent campaign to improve their lot by law, a campaign that wildly exaggerated the number of people involved, and the incidence of over-crowding and immorality amongst the boat population. These problems undoubtedly did exist, and his campaign did achieve a framework of regulations and regular inspections – backed by an official power to detain boats that did not conform to them – that set standards for cleanliness, overcrowding, paintwork and the physical condition of the cabin.

The legislation worked both ways, in theory at least, for the boatman could complain to the authorities that his boat was not fit to live in, and the boat owner could then be immediately compelled to do something about it. But it was a brave or foolish boatman in Victorian Britain who would choose to upset his employer and the owner of his home, in an age without any sort of employment protection. The canal inspectors were mainly regarded as an official nuisance, a cause of expense and unnecessary delay to be avoided if at all possible; but the existence of the laws did improve the basic situation. There were however always some squalid, unpainted boats with ignorant uncouth crews, lacking any pride in their lives or their trade. Disease, vermin and heavy drinking were constant com-panions to a small but significant part of the boating population, but as in most societies it appears that the great majority lay between the extremes of good and evil, working hard in reasonable boats with a modicum of pride and painted dec-oration to cheer their lives. Hanson sifts the mass of evidence carefully and con-cludes that after the Canal Boat Acts had made their improvements by the end of the century 'those who were in a position to know compared the boating class very favourably with workers of a similar class on land' *(Hanson, 1975)*.

Documentation of clean pretty boats with painted flowers did not figure strongly in the evidence of those who were seeking to prove the immorality of the boating class, or to improve their lot, but there was occasionally a more sympathetic if romantic view taken by some less didactic writers. The earliest pictorial illustration that offers a clear picture of the canal painting tradition as described by Hollingshead is a wood engraving that accompanies an article about the Thames in 1875. The author's opinion and description is worth quoting at length as a friendly contemporary view, roughly halfway through the canal age in England:

> The exterior decoration of these boats is noticeable, and evinces the pride taken in their appearance by their owners, who repaint them with the gayest colours as often as they can afford to do so. On the outside of the cabin are painted two or four landscapes (usually river scenes), of which they are proud enough. The one on the barge in our frontispiece is faithfully copied, and shows a river in which the water makes no attempt to find its own level, one side of the stream appearing many feet higher than the other. The tree might stagger a botanist, but the whole serves its first purpose as a cheerful decoration, which our more pretentious art so frequently misses. The smartness of the cabin part of the barge is often the more striking, from the fact that the load it bears is of a very opposite character, as coal, which is perhaps the most common freight.
>
> (ROBERTSON, 1875)

Pride of the Thames *is an illustration to* Life on the Upper Thames, *a compilation of articles by H. R. Robertson published in 1875 (initially published in the Art Journal of 1873). It provides some of the best pictorial evidence of the canal boat conventions of paintwork and costume of the period, and seems to prove that it was already a very well established tradition.*

*T*wo sketches from a page of illustrations entitled 'Life on Canal Boats', *published in 1884 in the* Illustrated Sporting and Dramatic News. *Both offer atmospheric glimpses of family boating and pictorial decoration on the cabin sides.*

This is clearly the same painted tradition that survived into the 1960s and is one that has been reasonably well documented and photographed since World War I. Prior to that the evidence gets progressively skimpier until we are back with Hollingshead in 1858.

There was a constant shadow looming over the boatmen of this period, for railway competition was threatening the prosperity of canal companies and the livelihood of the boat population. From the first experiments in South Wales in 1804, through the Stockton & Darlington Railway of 1825 to the opening of the Liverpool & Manchester Railway in 1830 – the first to compete directly with a waterway route – the threat to canal transport by steam locomotives on railways became increasingly clear. In fact the canal tonnage carried did not drop very dramatically at first, but the rates had to be cut to compete, so the income and dividends dropped considerably. So too did the boatman's wage.

There is little evidence to show what effect this had on the lives of the boat population. Increasing poverty of course, but did it affect their attitude to their trade, their pride in their calling, and did that call into being a body of imagery to call their own to re-state their presence? In many other trades the legalisation

of the unions, the grudging acceptance of workers' combinations as trade unions in 1825, resulted in a great wave of fraternal and communal visual art of public banners and private club regalia. This grew to a crescendo of popular pageantry throughout the nineteenth century with every trade union, friendly society and church Sunday school proclaiming their existence and importance to society on every public occasion possible.

Certainly there was very little organised union activity amongst the canal workers, but the pervading ethos of pictorial statements of working class solidarity was developing all round them as their traditional trade came under attack from developing industry. It would not be too surprising to find a visual language of protest and presence developing in this situation, but romantic landscapes and swags of flowers hardly seem to be the stuff of powerful statements of political intent. The traditional was theirs and theirs alone however, and it was proclaimed and brandished as a social statement like a miners' banner on Gala day. The painting was part of a whole visual language of ostentatious boat smartness – white-scrubbed wood, polished brasswork, with a brightly decorated water can set on the roof by the cabin chimney. Like the clean lace curtains and donkey-stoned doorsteps of the houseproud urban housewife it was a language both personal and public. It was a proud public statement of membership of a certain social group, but it was also a private display of standards for those in the know, the subtleties of which could only be appreciated by friends and rivals within the business. But why roses and castles, and where did they come from?

A fine set of well decorated narrow boats in Gloucester docks. Note the extraordinarily fancy gangplank stand on the boat on the right, with diamond patterns overlaid with rose panels, and a castle scene in the centre as well. Sabrina is also unusual in having a decorated water barrel on the cabin roof instead of a can, common practice on the Bridgewater Canal, but rare elsewhere.

CHAPTER 2

THE ROSE, AND THE CASTLE PICTURE

A watercolour by Philip Ballard of a boat cabin in 1838 assumed to be on the Herefordshire & Gloucestershire Canal, where his brother was the engineer. Ballard was a skilled china painter, and the other careful drawings in his delightful sketchbook suggest that this painting too is an accurate record of this boat, complete with flowers on the cabin side and a diamond pattern on the dog kennel, and therefore the earliest evidence of naturalistic painted decoration on canal boats to be discovered so far.

Roses are almost universally agreed to be beautiful in themselves, and are therefore a good symbol of beauty in the abstract as well. By an extension of that common understanding, anything decorated with roses is also perceived as being more beautiful, or is aspiring towards beauty, whether it be clothing, canal boats, or the Rose Queen's throne at the garden fête. A symbol so universally accepted must have touched more levels of emotion than simple visual pleasure to maintain its popularity so consistently over many generations and cultures, and so it proves. The white rose used to be used as a symbol of purity, and in Christian iconography often represented the Virgin Mary, the 'rose without thorns'; it is however the very viciousness of those thorns that gives meaning to the rose as an analogy of love and beauty in everyday human life. It is difficult to pick a rose without pain. A classical legend relates how the Goddess

Jan^ry 30th 1838

of Love pricked her foot on a white rose as she rushed to comfort her dying lover Adonis, and her passionate blood stained that white rose red for evermore. It is merely an ancient myth, but it still has an elemental power to touch the heart; and that same conjunction of thorns, blood and the white rose turned red has been absorbed into the legends surrounding the Crucifixion too.

The actual colour and shape of a rose, the gently unfolding petals embracing a deep secret heart is the key to its pre-eminence as the queen of flowers; but like all flowers, some of its poetic beauty is in its transience, the ephemeral nature of a beauty that buds, blooms and fades away in a few days or weeks, a touching parable of life. A rose in bloom speaks of summer warmth and youth, and painted flowers are a clutching attempt to preserve that moment and mood in perpetuity. This is quite understandable, and floral decoration and painted flowers appear universally as perhaps the commonest denominator of uncomplicated visual pleasure. If canal boats were going to be painted at all, then flowers were likely to be the most common image to be used, as they are throughout the folk arts of the world. In Britain many of those flowers would be roses.

Everything was far more complicated in the polite arts of the eighteenth century aristocracy, however, for every image had to be seen as an allegory, with hidden meanings to be understood by the classically educated. Thus flowers were allusions to certain saints or virtues, or were a metaphor for Love, for Venus, Cupid or Aphrodite; they could represent Springtime, Youth, Purity, or Passion and Martyrdom. Most of all they were simply tributes to Flora, Goddess of Flowers, a presiding spirit of Arcadia and pastoral simplicity, a set of mythical concepts that were popular with the leisured classes. Their money kept them firmly distanced from the reality of a mucky cowshed in an English winter, but their idealised poetic concept coloured the culture that was promoting the industrial revolution and the canals, and that Graeco-Roman fashion influenced everything.

'*Landscape with Psyche outside the Palace of Cupid*' was painted by Claude Lorraine in 1664, a fine example of his style of idealised landscape, now in the National Gallery, London. Despite the mythological title, it is mainly an atmospheric picture of light and imaginative architecture, more usually known simply as '*The Enchanted Castle*'.

It influenced the concept of landscape for example, both in reality and art. In reality it provided the incentive for the creation of the Palladian country house and the setting it was to be seen in, but the art of painting had already prepared the ground. Landscape painting as we now understand it, a picture of an interesting view worthy of being looked at for itself, is a quite recent invention. Before the seventeenth century, landscape painting was merely the background to something more important, a picture of an historical event, or a scene from classical mythology or the bible. Landscape was just countryside and weather you went through to get somewhere more interesting until one particular painter's work helped to change that perception, the paintings of Claude Lorraine.

Born in 1600, Claude was French, but spent most of his long life working in Italy where he developed a characteristic style of idealised classical landscape that became particularly popular with the visiting English aristocrats on their Grand Tours. A major part of an Englishman's formal education was a working knowledge of the classics, the myths and legends of the poetry of Homer and Virgil, the philosophy of Socrates and Plato, and a familiarity with the art and architecture of Ancient Rome. Much could be learnt from books, but a full appreciation of these values could only truly be absorbed in Italy itself, it was felt. The architectural ruins of the Roman Empire and the ancient marble statues had to be experienced under the Mediterranean sun, and a year or two's Grand Tour of the Continent became and remained an essential part of a gentleman's education for a couple of centuries. Like tourists today these aristocratic visitors wanted souvenirs of their travels. They collected art, and they commissioned artists to travel with them to record the journey; but in Italy the paintings that became most prized and most fashionable were the atmospheric landscapes of Claude and his host of copyists and followers. Ostensibly they are mythological or biblical pictures, 'Echo and Narcissus' or 'Hagar and the Angel', but actually they are pictures of place and mood, with the action of the title played out in the foreground by small figures who are relatively unimportant to the composition. Emotionally they sum up educated nostalgia for the distant past, for Arcadia, a

The Forum in Rome, one of the essential sights for the English visitors to Italy on their educational Grand Tours of Europe. This illustration is from a Victorian guide book.

A breadboard painted with a charming little castle picture by an unknown painter, now in Gloucester Folk Museum. Fitted with a neat little brass ring at the top, it presumably hung up on the wall when not in use to become part of the cabin decoration.

secular Garden of Eden. When brought back to Britain these pictures exerted a considerable influence on taste and fashion, an influence that continues in some form to the present day.

Claude landscapes are usually built to an almost theatrical formula of foreground wings, middle stage scenery and a backdrop. A dark foliage foreground with a tree or two rising on one side frames the view, where a classical temple or a ruinous castle in the middle distance hints at eons of human history, whilst the background sea and misty mountains lead the eye and imagination into a timeless luminous sky. This effective formula has been used, re-arranged and developed by numerous painters through the centuries; in the eighteenth century the most famous follower was probably the welsh artist Richard Wilson, although his wealthy patrons were in London; whilst in the nineteenth century it was Turner's turn, re-inventing the formula in many of his formal topographical works, and even painting one picture in direct artistic competition with another done by Claude nearly two hundred years before, just to prove he could do it. In all of them it is the man-made building in the middle distance set against the trees, hills and watery reflections of nature that provides the critical tension, the artistic balance of perennially popular art, including the castle pictures on canal boats. Turner would have been appalled.

At the height of the canal age, however, the purity of Claude's classical idealism had been diluted by several other strains of imagery and sentiment. It was the age of great country houses and of large scale landscape gardening where the physical reality of the parkland was re-arranged to look more fashionably attractive, to look more 'picturesque' in fact. This word has quite reversed its meaning over the years; where now we might see an interesting scene and describe it as picturesque, that it would make a good picture, in the eighteenth century they re-shaped their parks and gardens to look like existing pictures, and the pictures they wanted them to look like were the Italianate landscapes of Claude again, preferably with a building of some sort in the middle distance. Thus we get that plethora of garden temples and follies of the period, the additional architectural

*T*he sentimental romantic
view of rural life, as the
contented labourer returns to
his humble cottage, from a
Victorian anthology called All
round the Year.

ingredients that complete the composition of these artificial pictorial scenes. But Britain had also begun to recognise its own picturesque landscapes by this time, and our own gothic ruins, historic castles and lakeland scenery were at last recognised as attractive and aesthetically interesting in their own right. More particularly these scenes were often 'sublime', deeply affecting the gentle emotions cultivated by the fashionable poets and painters of the day who added their chorus of sentimentality to the general appreciation of landscape painting.

Another set of imagery was added to the landscape painter's palette by the work of George Morland, that of rustic simplicity and the humble but happy countrymen. Regardless of the miserable reality of country life for the poor, Morland's popular pictures of tumbledown stables and thatched cottages created an image of the country that was very acceptable to the urban middle class, picture-buying public, reacting against the squalor of expanding towns and industry. Rural poverty became an allegory of simplicity and purity, yet another manifestation of our constant underlying longing for that mythical Golden Age, of humanity before the Fall. With a combination of all these popular ingredients we are only a short step away from the melancholic ivy-clad ruins so popular with the Victorians or the hollyhock cottage with roses round the door of the 1930s. We are on the threshold of common taste, of popular art, of chocolate box and calendar pictures.

This imagery, these flowers and landscape paintings, were not specifically English or even British – they were and remain part of an international language. The concept of painting pictures of buildings in a landscape, particularly in the fairly formalised arrangements that we have been discussing, can probably be regarded as a narrow part of Western European art history; but flower decoration is very widespread, and any attempt to isolate or define the origins of the British canal boat decoration needs to be aware of that broad international field.

Unfortunately this awareness may confuse as much as clarify the situation, for two very different conclusions may be drawn from a widespread occurance of similar subject matter. If similar styles of formalised painted flowers only occurred on Scandinavian painted furniture and English canal boats we could tentatively but logically assume there was some connection, but they also occur in Russian, German, Dutch, Austrian and Swiss paintwork, on Portugese fishing boats, on Turkish ox carts and in America on Pennsylvanian Dutch tinware. Does this prove that all these folk arts stem from the same root, or that they are a unanimous and simultaneous satisfaction of a widely felt set of artistic needs? Are they similar visual answers to a universal question, like the sparks from an exploding firework, or a linked chain of cultural progress, one style of image begetting another elsewhere? Even if one searches for the more peculiar conjunction of rose and castle, or a combination of painted flowers and landscape pictures, the field is still quite wide. Much of the folk furniture of Northern Europe included pictures as part of their decorative scheme, and in Germany and Switzerland the subjects regularly include fantasy castles like those of the Rhine valley. Horse-drawn carts in Turkey still carry landscape pictures of lakeside scenery and sunsets as well as bold swags of flowers extraordinarily similar in technique and appearance to those on our canal boats. If some supporting evidence from another source were ever to emerge, a major wave of Turkish immigration to the English Midlands around 1800 for example, a strong case could be made for connecting the painting traditions. Much nearer to home was the decorative paintwork of Hinderloopen in the north-east part of the Netherlands, which is strikingly similar to that of the narrow boats in colour, technique and decorative usage. Bearing in mind that it was already established as a localised tradition in the eighteenth century and was only a good day's sailing barge trip from the Thames or the Humber, Hinderloopen paintwork must be the front runner as a possible foreign source, but once again we would need some complementary evidence to be sure. In the meantime it simply seems to be yet another international folk art response to an underlying need for quality.

A set of boat horse harness with painted decoration on the swingletree and the wooden bobbins that stop the traces chafing the horse's flanks. This set was used on the Trent & Mersey Canal and was recently discovered in store in a blacksmith's workshop near Sandbach, where it has been at least since the early 1950s.

A boat horse in working harness, but dressed up for the local horse show with extra brasses and crocheted ear caps. Frank Woodhouse at the head was a boatman with S. E. Barlow's fleet at Tamworth, but acted as company ostler at the weekends as well.

Possibly the closest foreign parallel to English canal boat painting to be seen at the end of the twentieth century is one that certainly did not exist in the nineteenth, that of the elaborate decoration of the motor lorries of India, Afghanistan and Bangladesh. All the component parts of the lorry cab and body are picked out in intense contrasting colours, and everything is smothered in patterns, floral and abstract, painted, carved, and nailed on in cut polished metal; most striking of all are all the pictures painted wherever there is a large enough space. There too are cottages and bridges, and sailing boats on tree-lined rivers and lakes, all painted against a lurid sunset sky. There are paintings of temples and the Taj Mahal, but these are in no sense nostalgic for they are equally matched with pictures of skyscrapers, railway locomotives, airliners and film stars. It is a vibrant hotch-potch of modern popular art imagery, unified by the slickness of the professional paintwork, an extraordinary flowering of decorative art on what are utilitarian tools for transport. They have become travelling icons of their own industry.

In Britain neither climate nor culture has encouraged the road transport industry to develop quite so decoratively, but there are hints that it could. Old-fashioned horse-drawn vehicle standards of coach painting, lining and elaborate signwriting are still used on motorway trucks as the finest way to advertise the reliability of a long established service, whilst for the driver there is the pride and pleasure of driving an immaculate and well maintained machine, and a sense of tradition. Several other aspects of modern lorry transport echo those of the old canal boats too; both are commercial cargo carriers with the captain or driver operating as an individual from a private compartment, in lorry cab or boat cabin. Both driver and boat captain also have considerable personal independence, for both can choose the way the job gets done once they leave the depot.

The similarity became closer during the 1970s and 1980s as the more wide-spread and official use of sleeper cabs encouraged the lorry to become home to the driver for an increasing proportion of his time. The personal additions to the cab increased, the ornaments inside, the extra lights and chromework on the outside, and a standard piece of transport equipment occasionally became customised to something far more individual. Here, too, paintings sometimes become part of the decorative scheme, ships in full sail, red indian warriors, girls of course, and on some Scottish lorries a kilted highlander in the heather against misty mountains. The parallels over two hundred years are thought-provoking.

The major social difference is the fact that the boatman often took his wife and children along with him, and in no other industry did a man's family work quite so constantly with him. This can easily be overstated, for all-male boat crews were very common, especially in the early days, and a majority of boat captains had a house ashore somewhere, even if his wife worked with him for a lot of the time. But we can surely assume that the boatwoman's taste and aspirations had a great deal of influence on the way her husband's boat was decorated.

The other major difference, and the most obvious, is the historic period in which these transport systems developed, for each draws its pictures and decorative techniques from its own contemporary life. Lorries and lorry drivers, whether English or Afghan, absorb their imagery from modern books, magazines, films and television. From what sources then might the canal boatman and his family have drawn their inspiration for their own occupational art?

B ess of Framilode loaded with coal from the Black Country for sale in the Gloucester area carrying the full complement of traditional decorations, with an unusual painting of a little boy on the cabin block.

CHAPTER 3

ORIGINS, POSSIBLE, PROBABLE AND PROBLEMATIC

The early nineteenth century boatman's contact with the art and imagery of educated society was much less in quantity, and far less immediate than our own, but perhaps that made his experience of pictures more meaningful. He was probably illiterate as were the majority of the population, but newspapers and magazines were sparsely illustrated anyway. Books illustrated with engravings were expensive, although the eighteenth century had seen a much greater availability of printed pictures for the poorer classes, and a consequent reduction in price. That was about to be accelerated dramatically by the invention of lithography, a good cheap printing process from re-usable stones, which quickly

The cabin-side castle panel of Montgomery (illustrated on page 40), a powerful painting, by an as yet unidentified painter.

A wooden box with a sloping hinged lid, perhaps used as storage for blacking brushes, and polish for boots or for the stove. The castle picture on the lid is in a fairly standard 'canal' style, but the formalised flowers on the front are more unusual and show great similarity to some japanned ware decoration.

developed into chromo-lithography and colour printing for the mass market – pictures for the wall, cards to post, and coloured packaging and advertising without end. That cheap ephemeral art of marketing was still to come, as was photography; mass production generally was still in its infancy.

However, our boatman and his family was more likely to come into contact with a wider range of hand craftsmen than we are today, including many painters both decorative and artistic. Society was complex and specialised, and every big town had its sign painters, carriage painters and heraldic painters, and even an ordinary house painter and decorator needed a wide range of skills with paint and brushes that we would now regard as artistic. There were also proper picture artists, painting portraits or landscapes to order, proportionately as many to a town as there might be photographers today. Some were good and some were bad, some expensive and others very cheap. The basic artistic skills to decorate the new canal boats were far more widely available to the boat owner than they would be in the twentieth century.

Different industries naturally demanded specialist decorators, and it is in the fast production of commercial goods that the main dissemination of high fashion ideas and imagery to the lower classes is most obvious. Cultured ideas were most likely to be transmitted to the provincial working man and woman through the work of a commercial decorator, whose job it was to convert fashionable taste into sales, and it is in the work of these commercial decorators that the closest parallels to the canal boat painting tradition occur.

There is often a clear conjunction of roses and castles on the painted dials of grandfather clocks for example. There are many other images used as well, ships, birds and emblematic ladies representing the four seasons or the four corners of the world, but a romantic picturesque castle is the favourite, supported by any number of varieties of flowers, with roses predominant. This imagery seemed a mere coincidence when first noticed; it was so far removed from canal boat

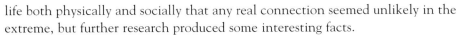

The full cabin side paintwork of Montgomery, *presumably photographed shortly after this boat entered the Samuel Barlow Coal Co. fleet from the Grand Union Carrying Co. in 1942, but the painting is quite noticeably different to the regular Braunston style employed by the Nurser boatyard which had been taken over by Barlow's by this time.*

life both physically and socially that any real connection seemed unlikely in the extreme, but further research produced some interesting facts.

The painted iron dial, white, with added decorations painted in the spandrels and on the semicircular arch above the clock face proper, was introduced between 1760 and 1780. Prior to that, long case clock dials were of brass, with engraved numerals and chapter rings, and the decoration was a mixture of engraving and added castings; the new white dials very quickly became popular with clockmakers and their customers, and the fashion was almost ubiquitous by 1820.

The surprise is that the great majority of them were both made and painted in the Birmingham area, regardless of the name and address on the dial, and were then exported to provincial clockmakers complete and decorated. The inevitable conclusion is that there was a numerous class of commercial painters of dials in business in the Birmingham area, which in turn meant that they were probably working within a few hundred yards of the canal. Although long case clocks were always significant investments, they were not then the expensive preserve of collectors or the middle classes only, but everyday equipment for many pubs and cottage homes. The paintings are often fairly crude in design or drawing, but the technique has usually become neat, fast and slick with practice, and it is clear that this style and taste in painted decoration would have been popular with the better class of working family, some of whom were taking to the

A long-case clock dial employing all the most common decorative motifs on one example: castles, cottages, ruins and flowers, with another landscape paired with a seascape on the dial at the top that shows the phases of the moon. It is almost a catalogue of the Midland clock dial painters' standard ingredients.

canal at this period. A connection between the two suddenly seems possible, if not exactly probable.

There was, however, another industry in the same area that employed even more artists for similar sorts of commercial decorative work, and that was the japanning industry. This produced a wide range of goods in tinplate and papier mâché, and finished them with a high gloss paint baked on in special ovens to achieve a very hard wearing surface. Everything was then elaborately embellished with designs, pictures and flowers, especially at its most productive period leading up to the Great Exhibition of 1851. Originally, japanning was an attempt to emulate the lacquer work imported in the seventeenth century from China and Japan (hence the name), but by the middle of the eighteenth century it was established as a proudly British business in South Wales and the Midlands. It continued to expand and employed hundreds of workers in

Wolverhampton, Bilston and Birmingham, a significant proportion of whom were very skilful painters. The range of goods produced was enormous in scale and quality, from entire aristocratic furniture suites in papier mâché to thousands of humble tin box or mantlepiece trinkets – flowers and pictures smothered everything. The designs used are a catalogue of the taste of the time, both fashionable and fairly humble. Sprays of flowers of all possible varieties (although roses usually predominated) had been popular on furniture since the time of Chippendale and Sheraton, and their popularity continued throughout the Victorian age on every variety of object. Pictures became popular currency as engravings of the work of famous artists became more readily available, and this taste for fine art was reflected in the japanning trade, for pictures appeared on everything – biblical pictures, hunting pictures, rustic scenes after Morland, dogs after Landseer, and picturesque landscapes without number. The academically sanctioned art of the educated elite percolated down to the lower classes through the medium of cheap mass-produced household items and ornaments – coal scuttles, tea caddies and thousands of tea trays.

It is time to return to Hollingshead once more, for his detailed description of the cabin paintwork:

> The Stourport is rather faded in its decorations, and is not a gay specimen of the fly-barge in all its glory of cabin paint and varnish; but still enough remains to show what it was in its younger days, and what it will be again when it gets a week in dock for repairs, at Birmingham. The boatman lavishes all his taste, all his rude uncultivated love for the fine arts, upon the external and internal ornaments of his floating home . . . The two sides of the cabin, seen from the bank, and the towing path, present a couple of landscapes, in which there is a lake, a castle, a sailing boat, and a range of mountains, painted after the style of the great teaboard school of art. (HOLLINGSHEAD, 1858)

A fluent Braunston style castle on the door from a butty cabin through to the hold, but probably not by Frank Nurser himself. It was found floating in the River Soar.

Teaboard is an old fashioned name for a tea tray, the most common product of the japanning industry, and with its flat central surface the most easily and commonly decorated. Hollingshead uses the expression 'the great teaboard school of art' in the same mocking but affectionate manner that we might use 'chocolate box art' to describe all those sentimental pictures of kittens, children, stage coaches and flower catalogue roses that try to talk us into buying them for granny's birthday present. It is common denominator art designed not to upset anyone. In Peggotty's houseboat in *David Copperfield* there was on the chest of drawers 'a tea tray with a painting on it of a lady with a parasol, taking a walk with a military looking child who was trundling a hoop . . . ' whilst in *The Old Curiosity Shop*, Dickens describes 'a gaudy tea tray, representing a lady in bright red walking out with a very blue parasol'. But the most popular commercial art of Hollingshead's experience was apparently the picturesque landscape of a castle by a lake. He continues:

> If the *Stourport* cannot match many of its companions in the freshness of its cabin decorations, it can eclipse every other barge on the canal in the brilliancy of a new two gallon water-can, shipped from a bank-side painter's yard, at an early period of the journey. It displayed no fewer than six dazzling and fanciful composition landscapes, several gaudy wreaths of flowers, and the name of its proud proprietor, Thomas Randle, running round the centre upon a background of blinding yellow. (HOLLINGSHEAD, 1858)

Here his description points to another close parallel to the japanning industry, if not exactly part of it, a piece of practical tinware, painted for protection, but elaborated to a rich state with paintings. Is it a coincidence that possibly the second most common product of the japanning trade were water jugs, not unlike a boat water can, but usually oval in section with a cranked pipe spout?

Canal water cans remained the boat people's pride and joy until the end of commercial carrying, and even the most sparsely decorated boats had them painted with a few roses. In latter days they were never as elaborately decorated as the one Hollingshead describes, but some that survive from the late nineteenth century, built by tinsmiths in a different technique to the later galvanised ones, have many more individual sections that create more boundaries for individual groups of flowers or pictures. One in a private collection in Weymouth has four separate castle paintings and seven groups of flowers, and the initials of the owner and the date 1903 running round the centre upon a background of bright red. Was the 'bank-side painter's yard' in Birmingham or Wolverhampton part of the general decorating industry of the Midlands? Did he paint water cans one day, and tea trays the next? The presence of so many decorators, using similar imagery, so close to the heart of the canal system during its most formative period, must surely suggest the japanning trade of the Midlands as a front runner in the debate about the origins of the canal boat tradition?

The other close contender must be the pottery industry which can also offer the right geography, imagery, and artists in the right historical period. There were major potteries alongside the canal at Worcester, Measham, London and Derby as well as all the Staffordshire Potteries which were for a while almost totally dependent on the Trent & Mersey canal to bring their raw materials in and to take away their finished products. Once again there were a large number of skilled painters employed in the industry, and presumably there were times when some became unemployed and available for other work. In 1848 the Crown Derby works closed and John Lead, one of the most skilled flower painters at Derby, decided to move to Davenport's at Longport. It is handed down as reliable family history that he moved house by canal, and paid for the

Two hand-painted mugs from Staffordshire, so similar to each other that they probably came from the same pottery, if not the same painter. The 1855 dated mug on the right commemorates the birth of William Beech, the son of a boatman who became a tunnel keeper at Saltersford.

removal trip by decorating the boat for the captain. There was also a regular interchange of painters between the japanning and ceramic industries at the high quality end of the market, and we can reasonably assume that there would have been a labour flow at the cheaper end as well.

The silly difficulty in some of these presumptions and suppositions is a lack of material evidence – silly because although we have inherited many of the expensive items, objects that have been looked after and dusted by careful servants for two hundred years, the much greater number of cheaper goods have long since been destroyed by the hard usage of an ordinary working life. We are left with an unbalanced body of evidence, country houses full of the antiques of the minority aristocracy, but with little to show what was in the back kitchens of the vast mass of working class society. We can only guess thoughtfully.

Thankfully this is less true of pottery, for if total breakage can be avoided glazed ceramics will last for a very long time, and the decorative brushwork of two centuries ago can still appear as fresh as the day it came out of the kiln. There were hundreds of craftsmen and women at work, and masses of examples of flower and landscape painting survive unscathed on pots and plates, beautiful professional painting techniques that offer an interesting comparison to the later boat painting methods. Flowers predominate as one would expect, but pictures featuring a building in a lakeside landscape feature strongly. Sometimes they are clearly an imaginative fantasy, but increasingly they became topographical pictures of real places, even if presented rather romantically. This is especially true after the production of Wedgwood's Queensware in the 1770s, a huge dinner and dessert service for fifty produced for Catherine II, Empress of Russia, each piece of which featured an individual painting of a famed British landmark, building or beauty spot. Josiah Wedgwood, with his strong flair for publicity, exhibited this whole ennobling set of decorated creamware in his showroom in London before export; it created a sensation, and a whole new imitative fashion in this very competitive business. Churches, castles, great houses and ruins all became part of the fashionable yearning after the picturesque.

The practical economics of large scale pottery manufacture meant that the concept of mass production came early to the potteries, and they were especially receptive to any process that could speed up the decoration as well. The 1750s saw the invention of transfer printing onto pottery, a process which is still the basic principle of much commercial ceramic decoration. Designs were engraved on copper and printed onto thin paper in the normal way. The print was then stuck face down onto the earthenware pot after its first firing, the paper was washed off to leave the ink behind, and another firing was given to permanently fix the printed design. Then it was dipped in glaze and fired for a third time to give it the final 'glost' hard wearing finish. Initially it was one company in Liverpool that controlled the process and contracted to decorate china ware for several potteries, but the technique spread rapidly and by 1800 many Staffordshire potteries were doing their own under-glaze printed decoration and the process was expanding rapidly down-market.

Blue and white was very popular and remains so today. It started in emulation of the imported porcelain of China which had been in great demand for a hundred years, and the marriage of blue and white with the Orient found its most pervasive expression in the ubiquitous Willow Pattern design of about 1780 but all other standard decorative images were reproduced almost ad infinitum.

Flowers abound – roses, carnations, camellias and chrysanthemums, both as a central picture on a plate and entwined amongst running foliate borders around everything. There were landscapes of every variety both real and imagined although many of them incline towards a vaguely Italianate pastoral theme, with shepherds tending their flocks in the shade of romantically overgrown classical ruins. Once more we are back under the all pervading influence of Claude Lorraine: 140 years after his death, Wedgwood marketed a new design in 1822 simply entitled 'Claude', whilst their 'Corinthian Temples' design is clearly based on one of his compositions.

This multitude of transfer printed designs are not hand painting of any sort, but they do illustrate the widespread fashion, obsession even, amongst all classes with the image of a romantic landscape, the building, the mountain and the lake. Hollingshead's 'teaboard school of art' was on the cups and saucers as well as the tray, and we can be confident that the boatmen who were carrying these goods in bulk would have had their own cupboards well equipped with nicely decorated china from all the rejects available at source, if not from the odd crate that was accidentally broken open.

There is one further area of popular art that would seem by its similarity of subject matter and commercial approach to be related to the canal boat tradition. Cheap landscape paintings on glass appeared in considerable numbers sometime during the mid-nineteenth century, and because of the permanence of the technique – the paint is applied directly to the back of the picture glass – they have survived in large numbers. Nearly all are 24 inches by 16 inches (60

An early nineteenth century meat dish with typical blue underglaze transfer printed landscape design featuring castle, cottage and rustic serenity.

An early Victorian glass painting, painted in reverse on the back of the picture glass with almost breathtaking commercial crudity. The freshness of the colours and the professional verve of the paintwork made them very attractive in their brashness however, and good surviving examples of the popular taste of the times.

by 41 centimetres), mounted in a maple veneered bolection moulded frame with a gilt slip. The great majority exactly fit the landscape formula as defined by Hollingshead – the mountains, castle or cottage, trees and lake, complete with sailing boats in the distance. Many of them are almost unbelievably bad and crude in execution, yet because they are done with such commercial verve and the colours retain their original gaudy freshness they are still superficially attractive, like brash seaside souvenirs or Staffordshire figures.

Their origin is as yet unknown. Antique dealers like to call them German, but with no supporting evidence, and it seems more likely they are part of the British interest in picturesque landscape. But they were certainly cheap, as witnessed by the evident speed and crudeness with which they were done, and were thus part of the working class taste of the time, a taste and fashion that we can assume the more respectable boating population to have shared or aspired to. The actual hanging of such pictures within the cabin was clearly impractical, but the direct painting on the walls and furniture of the panelled and moulded cabin would have been an easy step to make. This is all conjecture, however, and far away from proper evidence.

What is clear is that at the time the canals were at the peak of their prosperity as boat building was expanding and more boat crews were being recruited, there was in existence a range of industries and a widespread fashion of common imagery that could easily have provided both the designs and the craftsmen for the earliest narrow boat decoration. Lacking any other hard evidence this fashion and these English industries and opportunities seem to me to be a very persuasive argument for a local origin to the boat tradition. A foreign one is possible, but improbable.

There remains the enigma of Arthur Atkins who said he started it. He retired from work with the Oxford Canal Company in 1914 after sixty three years' faithful service without, according to one of the newspaper reports, having 'committed any act to call for a reprimand from his superiors'. He was by then the district agent for the Coventry and Oxford Canal Companies, living and working at Hawkesbury Stop, but when he started work at the age of twelve he was employed as a clerk in the office at Braunston.

Dickens called there in the course of his tour of the Grand Junction and Oxford Canals. He was accompanied by the famous Leigh Hunt, and in the office Dickens noticed a canal boatman's water-can which Atkins had been painting for a man named Randle. The novelist expressed a wish to possess one, and the subject of this notice executed a commission. In an article on inland canals, Charles Dickens subsequently mentioned the painted water-can, and not to the disadvantage of Mr Atkins either. Mr Atkins is probably the first man who ever painted a canal boatman's water can, and he had the vessel made from patterns by a tinplate work-er named Thwaites at Daventry, and afterwards painted it with landscapes and flowers.   *MIDLAND DAILY TELEGRAPH, Wednesday 22 July, 1914*

A pair of water cans dated 1896, which originally belonged to a Gerald Soames, whose name is just visible around the centre band. They both appear to be painted by the same painter, who employs a wide range of recognisable flowers to decorate them. The can on the left has a continuous castle landscape running right round the upper part, of which the sailing boat visible here is just one part.

A close-up view of some of the unusual but attractive flowers on a 1902 water can. It appears that the older the can, the greater the variety of flowers that are likely to be used.

The following day a rival newspaper (untraced as yet because the article only survives as a dated cutting) repeats the story, some of it word for word the same, but it does seem to refer back to its own archives and journalists, for it elaborates the story considerably and says 'Mr Atkins has been a frequent contributor to this journal as a correspondent of "Spectator in Warwickshire", and "Spectator" once enquired for a friend how it came to pass that the buckets and utensils used by canal people were always so brilliantly painted. Mr Atkins sent the reply that he painted the first boatman's water can and detailed the circumstances'. What then follows is the same Dickens anecdote, but with many additions.

Atkins it seems was something of an artist, even at that young age, and when Dickens and his companion asked for directions to the Four Crosses the lad showed them some sepia sketches he had made of the famous hostelry, so that they would recognise it. They were impressed. As Dickens was going out 'he noticed what is known as a boatman's kettle which had been painted by Atkins, and he enquired of what use it was. Atkins explained that it served a double purpose: on one side was a picture, and when hung up it served as an ornament; the other side was blank, and was used to place the kettle on when the boatman's family was at meals. These kettles are made of wood, and are familiar to anyone acquainted with the fittings of a boat. Dickens was very much struck with the affair and calling in the captain of the boat, a man named William Randle, better known as *Bonkey*, Dickens told him if he liked the kettle he would buy it for him. Randle said he should like it very much, and Dickens gave young Atkins two shillings for it, and presented it to Randle'.

In the common tradition of hack journalism, these newspaper articles were resurrected and regurgitated without acknowledgement into the *Oxford Times* thirteen years later in 1927 when they reported Arthur Atkins' funeral at Worcester, and yet again into the *Coventry Standard* in June 1939 in a general article about the Coventry Canal.

It could of course all be true, and the search for the origin of the canal boat tradition would be over, but there are a number of inconsistencies that leave some lurking doubts. There seems no reason to disbelieve most of the basic facts of the story, apparently told by Arthur himself to *Spectator of Warwickshire*. Arthur says he was seventeen or eighteen years old at the time of his meeting with the illustrious novelist, which would have been around 1858. Was this before or after the publication of Hollingshead's 'Household Words' article? Was it perhaps this visit to Braunston that suggested to its editor that the subject of canals, and their painted boats, was worthy of a series of articles? Why did Dickens 'call in the captain of the boat, William Randle'? Was Dickens travelling by boat? Is it the same captain Randle that Hollingshead travelled with, designated Thomas Randle on his newly painted water can? If Atkins was the first to paint up a water can, presumably within the preceding few years since starting work, why does Hollingshead write in a way that suggests they are common? Why are we unable to find that mention of a painted can in the work of Charles Dickens that 'was not to the disadvantage of Mr Atkins either'?

There is also something of a puzzle about the job Arthur Atkins was employed to do when he was working in the offices at Braunston, because 'as well as doing his work for the canal company he was devoting a considerable proportion of his time to sketching and painting at which he was considered very clever'. By the time he retired he had sent sketches of local interest to *Spectator*; the *Telegraph*

said 'as an amateur artist he has achieved some distinction', whilst the *Oxford Times* remarked that 'many houses in the neighbourhood of Coventry contain various paintings in oils from his brush'. This obituary also says that he showed artistic ability as a schoolboy, which suggests a relatively well-to-do upbringing, although the fact that he started work at twelve years old alludes to a humbler background. Census returns for the period show that his father was a toll clerk, and their previous addresses in the area suggest that he too worked for the Oxford Canal Company. Did Arthur come in after school to help his father as a part time office boy, or was he fully employed by the company as a clerk? Or humbler still, was he perhaps employed as a painter in the boatyard next door?

Unfortunately most of the information we have seems to emanate from Arthur himself, as told to *Spectator of Warwickshire*, and some quite different interpretations can be put on the evidence depending on what attitude the reader thinks that Atkins had towards himself and his achievements. It may all be true, but Atkins was an old man when he retired, and if he was prone to the sort of editing of the past to which old men are often tempted, re-telling stories to show themselves in the best possible light without much likelihood of being refuted, then an alternative version could be proposed that fits the facts. Suppose that Arthur Atkins reads the article in *Household Words* magazine some time after it is published. The author's name was not mentioned in the magazine itself, but it was clearly edited by Charles Dickens, and it would have been an easy mistake to assume that he also wrote a considerable amount of it. Atkins remembers Hollingshead and his companion Cuddy coming to Braunston with Captain Randle, remembers selling them a can and a kettle, remembers posting letters for them, but makes the assumption that the one was the famous Charles Dickens, and presumes the other was Leigh Hunt. Here is the basis of a good story to tell your grandchildren, and gullible journalists later in life. The unnamed author in *Household Words* certainly did mention the 'brilliancy of a new two gallon water can, shipped from a bankside painters yard at an early period in the journey' painted with landscapes and flowers. Thus far it is a simple misunderstanding, but when Atkins says that he was the first man who ever painted a canal boatman's water can, a more profound doubt is born. It sounds like deliberate self-aggrandisement by a self-satisfied and self-opinionated old man. But who was going to argue with him after sixty years, at the height of his retired respectability?

This sceptical view of Mr Atkins' own account may be much too harsh, for some of the unnecessary details of the story would seem to provide strong circumstantial evidence to support his case. He actually remembered that Dickens left five letters to be posted at the Braunston canal office, and remembered the names and addresses of four of them, including George Eliot. 'Dickens gave him a shilling to cover the postage, and told him he could keep the change'. Arthur Atkins had quite a lot of conversation with Dickens and his companion '. . . a gentleman who Mr Atkins thinks was Leigh Hunt . . .' and as Charles Dickens was so famous by then, it was surely unlikely to have been a case of mistaken identity. If only that article on inland waterways in which Dickens mentioned the painted water can were not so elusive, one could be more confident of the truth of the story. Until then Arthur Atkins remains an enigma.

The newspaper photograph of Mr Arthur Atkins published in 1914 when his retirement was announced in the Midland Daily Telegraph *after 63 years with the Oxford Canal Company.*

CHAPTER 4

THE PROFESSIONAL PAINTERS – ALL IN A DAY'S WORK

This introduction to some of the individual boat painters has to be begin with something of an apology for incompleteness, and some very hazy statistics. It would be very satisfying to be able to offer the names and details of all of the men involved in the business, but in fact even the number involved must be something of a 'guesstimate'. During the twentieth century there have been at least thirty-five canal boatyards in operation whose main business was the construction and repair of long-distance narrow boats, and possibly many more.

*B*raunston-style paintwork at its best: the work of Frank Nurser on the cabin side of the Samuel Barlow Coal Company boat Forget me Not *in the 1940s.*

In addition there were at least forty yards on the Birmingham Canal Navigations which concentrated on the open 'day' or 'joey' boats of the area, but many of them docked cabin boats as well. If there were only one man per yard capable of painting roses and castles we can already presume at least seventy men have been so employed as part of their job, but in fact a detailed knowledge of a few of these yards shows that at any one time there were often two or three trades-men capable of doing the decoration, even if only one of them was regarded as the specialist. Perhaps we could very conservatively round that figure up to eighty boatbuilder-painters. There were in addition the host of barge-building yards on the rivers and broad canals that fed and connected the narrow canals to the sea, and all of those could and would dock and paint narrow boats if nec-essary. There too were men who could turn out a respectable castle and a bunch of roses. Could we add another ten men to our list?

If a tradesman's full working life was fifty years, then one can certainly double the number of painters arrived at so far to cover the century from the 1850s to the 1950s, and the tradition could of course be fifty years older than that. Assuming that our number of boatyards represents the average throughout the canal age, which is unlikely, the most conservative possible estimate of the num-ber of men professionally engaged in the business of our subject must be 180, and it seems very likely to be double that. So far I have only managed to isolate the identity of forty-one individual painters, and some of those are no more than a name remembered by a workmate or a boatman, and in one case is just a signature on a cabin block. Clearly more work needs to be done, but progress in discovering new names and information has now slowed down to a pace that suggests that the facts so far available may now be offered as a useful proportion of the information that will ever be unearthed. Is this presumptuous? In some ways I hope so, for such a fascinating tradition deserves a more satisfactory conclusion than I can offer at present.

What follows therefore is only a narrow sample of the boat painters, dictated mainly by the availability of the memories of those that knew them, and any deductions from this sample can only really be regarded as valid to relatively recent history. Despite this disclaimer I hope the reader will find much of inter-est and value in this selection of short histories, an illustration of a valuable interaction between craftsmanship, applied art and real life. We just need to remember that these named individuals represent many more who are now lost in the anonymity of canal boat history.

Because boat painting came to be regarded as a part of boat building, it followed that it also became an almost exclusively male occupation. Once it was established as an historically masculine trade, even against all logic, it would have taken a very brave or stubborn woman to break into it, and in the con-ventional world of canal life women were far too conservative (and generally overworked) to want to take much interest. Even amongst the boat people who took it up as a hobby, women were in a tiny minority, whilst Matilda Woodhouse is the only female professional canal painter recorded by name. She painted water cans, and presumably other boat equipment as well, for sale in her uncle's canalside general store at Long Buckby top lock which he opened in 1920, and she seems to have built up a considerable reputation. Her work was so good (or was so cheap) that she was kept in full-time employment in a small workshop in a caravan behind the autocratic Jimmy Lovelock's shop, where she spent a great

The table cupboard flap from a cabin decorated by Frank Nurser at Braunston, a very typical example of his later work.

*D*ecoration and lively
lettering by Frank Nurser
on the motor boat Winston,
built new at Braunston in
1940. This could be its first
painting, for it was soon
to change its name to Alec
following a fatal accident
involving a child from
this boat.

deal of her increasingly miserable life. Born in 1906, Matilda committed suicide
before she was thirty years old, leaving men to completely dominate the business,
until the holiday industry introduced a whole new generation of decorative
painters to the canals.

The successful survival of the boat painting tradition is partly due to the basic
painting technique, one simplified over the years to a system that is relatively
easy to learn and remember, a system that is decoratively successful and so quick
to do that it remained affordable. One important factor in the development of
that traditional technique was the standard boatbuilder's apprenticeship, the
master to pupil relationship between an older craftsman and a young beginner.
Teaching 'art' was not in question. The art teacher develops the pupil's awareness of art as a concept in the abstract, trying to develop the youngster's own
aesthetic sense, after which he or she will create their own new individual work.
In the boatyard the master craftsman's duty to his apprentice is to try to train him
to be as good a workman as himself, or better – although this can create jealousy

and be a blow to his pride. The obvious road to this end is to train him to do the job in exactly the same way. Concurrently, the apprentice's duty is to respect the older man's experience, and to copy his methods until he can do it as well as the master, or better, when he is likely to get very cocky. Both men, young and old, are pushing towards a state where their work should be indistinguishable, and in the craft of canal boat painting this can lead to considerable confusion when trying to identify the work of individual men, especially as they never expected it to be judged individually anyway. It was the reputation of the boat-yard that mattered.

Nevertheless, however hard one person tries to copy another's work there will be differences of abilities and variations of techniques, and ultimately a difference of internal aesthetics – that personal sense of what looks 'right' and is acceptable. After a few years' experience and practice these personal variations will have become a painting style that is as individual as a signature, even though the pictorial ingredients are the same. The works of some painters can be clearly recognisable by their personal style, even though their names may not yet be known, whilst in other cases the boatyard pedigree of a particular piece of paintwork can be distinguished by style, and hence its authorship tentatively postulated. It is an inexact science, but fun.

M*aster painter Frank Nurser signwriting the* motor boat Tiger *at Braunston dock in August 1950.*

BRAUNSTON
AND
TAMWORTH

A cabin block, a seatboard and a massive stool built as an engine room step, all decorated at Nurser Brothers boatyard at Braunston.

One of the most outstanding canal artists of the twentieth century was Frank Nurser of Braunston, and he is almost certain to remain the most famous. To a large degree this is because his work was extremely good – lovely colours, involved compositions of flowers and confident handling of the paint, which the photographs will illustrate much better than words; but there are a number of

A set of decorated running blocks, used to guide the long butty towing rope back from the mast to a T stud on the cabin roof. This set was painted by George Crowshaw at Braunston in the 1950s.

other contributory elements to his reputation which also need discussing. Geographically, for example, the Nurser boatyard at which he worked all his life was in a good position to become well known, at the crossing of the major canal routes between London, Birmingham, Oxford, and the Coventry coalfields. This was the heart of 'Number One' country, the owner boatmen who set the highest standards of decoration and fancy painting, and Braunston village has been home to a large number of boat families since its earliest canal days. Pickfords had a warehouse and a boatyard there soon after the Grand Junction was completed in 1805 and by the end of the nineteenth century the largest canal carrier, Fellows, Morton & Clayton, had a major transhipment depot there.

Frank's fame, however, rests more on the events of the middle of the twentieth century when canals and their colourful populations were brought to the public's attention by Tom Rolt's book, *Narrow Boat*, nationalisation, and the Inland Waterways Association. Braunston was on the busiest narrow boat route, and the Grand Union Canal naturally became the focus for much of the media attention, with its direct connection to London. Photographers and commenta-

Nelson, *a motor boat previously owned by Charles Nelson and Co of Stockton, being signwritten and decorated by Percy Foster at Braunston just before World War II.*

tors all loved the quaint boats and their painted castles, and not unnaturally sought out the best known practitioners of the art. Frank Nurser was perfect, a craftsman of the old school maintaining the boat traditions with great skill in a family boatyard whose buildings and atmosphere seemed timelessly Olde English. Although spoken of as a quiet and shy man, he seemed to take to his new role as a national living treasure, as one of England's last true folk artists with perfect ease and confidence during the last few years of his life.

Some of this reputation devolved from a friendship with Rolt, for it was Rolt who made the recommendation that the Nurser boatyard should be the background for some of the film, *Painted Boats*, and that a Nurser-painted boat, the *Sunny Valley* should be the star of the film. This was made in 1944 and released to critical acclaim in 1945. Nurser appeared on television in 1948 demonstrating his craft to Susan Woolfit and presenter Joan Gilbert, and his work and his photograph appeared in Rolt's *Inland Waterways of England*, published in 1950 and in Barbara Jones' *Unsophisticated Art* of 1951. Frank Nurser died in 1952, but his style and influence live on in the number of examples of his work he left behind, in the work of those he taught, and in the respect and friendship of all those that knew him.

His father, William Nurser, began the family business in about 1875, but it is quite likely that he took over an existing boatyard, perhaps the one recorded in 1801 as belonging to a Mr Hughes, but there is as yet no evidence of how William acquired the skill or the money to set up in business. His father Thomas was a canal labourer, and had been born in the next village of Welton, which

suggests a long family connection to the area, although William himself was born near Tamworth in 1837. He married Clara when he was twenty-four and they set about rearing a large family, two daughters and eight sons, several of whom worked with their father in the boatbuilding business. Not content with this dynasty he married again after Clara died in 1880, and fathered two more children, of whom Frank was the youngest, born in 1886. William Nurser died in 1899 aged sixty-two, just as Frank started his apprenticeship, and the boatyard passed on to the eldest son of the first family, William Thomas Nurser, twenty-four years Frank's senior. He too brought his sons into the business. From the skimpiest records it would seem that the William Nurser company continued for a number of years quite satisfactorily for it employed a fair number of men (six of them Nursers) until after World War I. Then there was a sharp decline, whether due to bad management or the economic recession of the time, and the boatyard closed in 1927 and remained closed and empty for a short period. Finally Frank, with one of his younger half-brothers, Charles, and the black-smith Thomas Hitchman, formed a three-way partnership, bought the boatyard and opened as Nurser Brothers in 1928, a business that continued quite success-fully until bought out complete by the Samuel Barlow Coal Company in 1941. Even then things did not change very radically because, although Charles retired, Frank stayed on as the manager of the Barlow-owned boatyard, and remained the main decorator and signwriter.

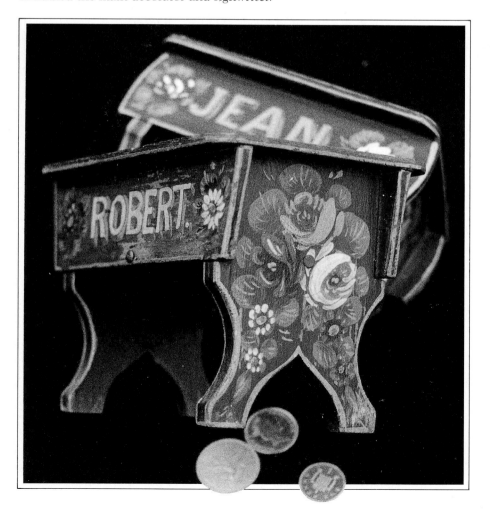

Two of a set of three miniature stool moneyboxes made by Walter Hollis, a boatbuilder at Nurser Bros, for his grandchildren Jean, Robert and Susan, and decorated by Percy Foster in 1944.

Frank gave the impression to several people who spoke to him in later life that he learnt how to paint from his father, but that teaching must necessarily have been quite brief in proper tradesman's terms, as he was only fifteen when his father died. He would however have been messing around in the boatyard as a child, watching his father and elder brothers at work, and we can assume that much of William senior's paintwork would have stayed in existence for several years following his death as an example for the young apprentice painter. What will probably remain unclear is what his father's style of paintwork was like, and how much Frank's style followed any sort of family pattern. It is also interesting to speculate whether there was any cross-influence between the paintings of Arthur Atkins in the canal office and the work of young William Nurser in the boatyard. They must surely have been acquainted, and might even have been close friends for thirty years.

When the boatyard re-opened as Nurser Brothers they took on a local lad as apprentice, Percy Willsworth Foster, who continued to work there until his

*E*ngine room side door painted in 1967 by Jess Owen, the painter at Charity Dock, Bedworth, in his typical dashing style.

Details of the rose painting of Percy Foster on a tunnel lamp, virtually indistinguishable in style to that of his tutor, Frank Nurser. Unusually this object is dated and signed on the back (Nov. 22 1945 P.W. F.) just months before he died. Perhaps he was becoming more conscious of his failing health and wanted to make his mark before it was too late.

tragically early death from tuberculosis in 1945. He became an extremely accomplished decorator and signwriter, and some who knew his work thought that he was better than Frank Nurser – praise indeed. What is significant is that such a small yard employing only seven or eight men should need two decorative painters in the workforce at the time. Frank was the business manager, and necessarily spent some of his time in the office, but it was perhaps the concentration on repair work that demanded a higher proportion of painting work than in earlier, more prosperous days. Fewer new boats were being ordered, boats needing six or eight weeks concentrated timber work to a week of painting, replaced by regular repair work that might only need a few days' boatbuilding and carpentry work to the same week for painting. Add to that the reputation that the Nursers had built up for producing a beautifully painted boat for their finicky owner-boatman customers and the balance is more understandable.

The company's fortunes became quite closely bound up with those of the Samuel Barlow Coal Company who came to rely heavily on Nurser's to maintain their fleet. They had their own boatyard near Tamworth, the 'Limited' dock as it became known to distinguish it from S.E. Barlow's boatyard nearby, concentrating mainly on their open boats running up into the Birmingham Canal network. The long-distance family boats came increasingly to Braunston for docking as the Samuel Barlow's fleet expanded in the 1930s. Some were built new, but a majority were bought in from other carriers, a significant proportion of which were the boats of the owner-boatmen, old Nurser customers anyway. Their business had suffered badly when the Grand Union Carrying Company secured the coal contracts to the paper mills at Nash, Apsley and Croxley, and many of them sold out completely to Barlow's, who had in any case been acting as their traffic agents for some of their business. Most continued to work the same boats under Barlow's management.

It is a little surprising, but refreshing, that Barlow's did not try to economise by reducing the amount of painted decoration that was professionally applied to their fleet. In fact photographic evidence suggests that the amount of fancy work increased during the 1930s, perhaps under some pressure from their new

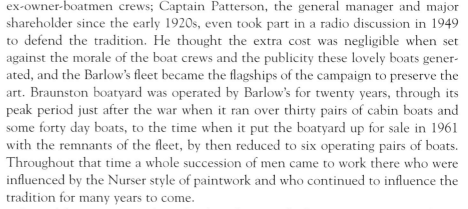

George Crowshaw decorating a water can at Barlow's Braunston boatyard in July 1957, where he was the yard foreman and chief decorator following Frank Nurser's death in 1952.

ex-owner-boatmen crews; Captain Patterson, the general manager and major shareholder since the early 1920s, even took part in a radio discussion in 1949 to defend the tradition. He thought the extra cost was negligible when set against the morale of the boat crews and the publicity these lovely boats generated, and the Barlow's fleet became the flagships of the campaign to preserve the art. Braunston boatyard was operated by Barlow's for twenty years, through its peak period just after the war when it ran over thirty pairs of cabin boats and some forty day boats, to the time when it put the boatyard up for sale in 1961 with the remnants of the fleet, by then reduced to six operating pairs of boats. Throughout that time a whole succession of men came to work there who were influenced by the Nurser style of paintwork and who continued to influence the tradition for many years to come.

Part of this process was brought about by a much closer co-operation with the other Samuel Barlow dock at Amington Road, Tamworth, the 'Limited' dock. This had been set up during World War I, mainly to build and service the company's open coal boats, but they docked and painted many of the cabin boats as well. When George Baxter started work there in the early 1920s the foreman of the yard was Len Shakespeare, a man who had served his time at Lees & Atkins dock at Poleworth, which will be discussed in more detail later. He was a good painter and signwriter apparently, the best that George could remember, but this might be just loyalty to the man that taught him his trade. After working at Rickmansworth for a short period before World War II, George returned to the

'Limited' dock, and was one of several men transferred to Braunston for a while. He lived and worked there continuously for twelve months, but others travelled by train from Tamworth as the need arose.

After the death of Percy Foster in 1945 there was a distinct hole in the Nurser workforce, and George Crowshaw, by this time the foreman on the 'Limited' dock spent an increasing amount of time working at Braunston. When Frank finally retired, and died soon afterwards in 1952, it was George Crowshaw who continued as the dock foreman and main decorative painter at Braunston during the last years of the Samuel Barlow Coal Company. He too had served his time at Polesworth, working alongside his father Edward, and although he seems to have shaped his paintwork into the Nurser mould very closely, by this time almost the Samuel Barlow trademark, his castle pictures show some distinctly Polesworth ingredients.

Seventeen-year-old apprentice Ron Hough decorating a cabin block and can at Barlow's dock in 1949.

The trip boat Water Ouzel, *with roses and castles done by Dennis Clarke in the 1970s, when he owned and operated it in Braunston. It was photographed in 1993 just prior to a major restoration which required the complete replacement of these cabin sides.*

Yet another boatbuilder to come under the Nurser influence was Jess Owen, who came to Braunston in 1948 after working for some years in the Black Country, servicing open canal boats. He had done his apprenticeship in the Staffordshire Potteries before the war, but only took to the decorative paintwork whilst he worked for Barlow's, under Frank Nurser. It was when he moved on to work at Charity Dock at Bedworth that his style really blossomed, especially in the mid-1950s when many of the boats of the emerging Willow Wren fleet were put into commission and beautifully decorated there. He continued to practise his traditional trade at the Gilbert Bros dock right through to an early retirement from ill-health. He died in 1990 aged sixty-seven.

As well as influencing these painters who were already in the trade, Frank employed two lads soon after the war to learn the job from scratch, a younger generation of painters to carry the tradition forward. In 1946 Dennis Clarke joined Barlow's as an apprentice boatbuilder and quickly became an accomplished decorator, although he never became a confident signwriter. His father, the publican of the Admiral Nelson at Braunston for many years, was a nephew of Frank's, the son of one of his sisters, so a tenuous family connection was also being maintained. Dennis was only a few years younger than Frank's own son Peter, and they both spent much of their childhood around the boatyard before being formally employed there. In 1949 National Service intervened, but he returned to Barlow's afterwards for another couple of years. Things were changing however, for traffic was declining, Patterson's management was taken over by Raymond Stephens in 1951, and Frank died in 1952. Dennis left in 1953, but after various jobs away from the canal, he eventually returned to work for the

A pair of cabin doors from the hotel boats Rose *and* Castle, *with confident Braunston style decoration by Dennis Clarke. They probably date from their first working season in 1970, when he owned the boats, but are now honourably retired in the offices of the boats' present owners at Rugby.*

young Willow Wren company at their dockyard premises at the Bottom Lock at Braunston. Here he became dock manager and took up the brushes again to decorate their optimistically expanding fleet, and some of his work survives from this period. He stayed with the company as a manager and director as it later diversified into hire cruisers and hotel boats. Although the carrying company was wound up in 1970, the other businesses under new names still operate, and some of their boats still carry Dennis's flamboyant roses and simple but supremely confident castles. He died in 1990.

In 1950, with Dennis away in the army, the 16-year-old Ron Hough started work at the Barlow's dock as a general boat builder. Although he was from a boating family, he had spent his whole childhood in Braunston village and was very familiar with the boatyard. Ron quickly showed a preference and an undoubted talent for painting, and worked with Frank Nurser very closely for

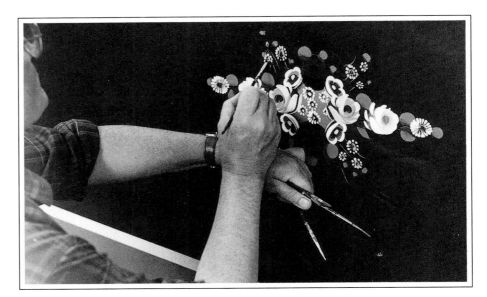

The professional practised skill of Ron Hough magically creating his typically flamboyant flowers in 1993.

two years before he was drafted for National Service. Frank's teaching was very thorough and practical and Ron was an enthusiastic student, and he learned to paint in a style that was almost indistinguishable from his master's for a while, although it soon developed an individualism that became the unmistakable Hough trademark, with glorious arrangements of loose-petalled roses in full summer bloom, crisply painted with neat dexterity.

When he returned from the army, Ron worked at a variety of jobs before the opportunity arose to return to boat painting as an almost full-time painter in 1962. The pleasure boat business boom was well under way, and the Barlow's boatyard was bought out by Michael Street as a base for Blue Line Cruisers, his developing hire boat company, and his hotel boats *Nancy* and *Nelson*. He also bought the remains of the carrying fleet and their contracts, and it is to his great credit that he continued to maintain these boats to a high standard until these contracts were terminated abruptly in 1970. Although remaining self-employed, Ron Hough became the regular decorative painter at the ex-Barlow's dock, and helped to keep the ex-Barlow's coal boats looking immaculate to the end of their working lives.

He also helped Michael Street develop a very strong business in the supply of painted ware as souvenirs to the holiday trade, and it has perhaps been under-estimated how important this business was to the survival of the traditional art during those critical years just after World War II. Once more we are probably in debt to Tom Rolt, and to his close friendship with Anthony Heal, for it was Heal's famous store in London that provided the venue for the IWA's first Inland Waterway exhibition in 1947, one that then went on to tour the country. And it was Heal's which placed a regular contract for the supply of painted ware to its Tottenham Court Road shop from Nurser's at Braunston. This contract provided encouragement and extra money for all the Braunston painters, from Frank himself, through George Crowshaw, Jess Owen, Dennis Clarke, to Ron Hough, who was still supplying Heal's in Michael Street's early days. It was becoming less important by then, for there were many more canal shops to sell to, and many more canal enthusiasts keen to preserve the tradition, but without that extra cash incentive to the painters to do it in their spare time as well as at work, there may have been much less painting produced, less skill developed, and less tradition passed on. The down side to this commercial development was the

emergence of a class of souvenir painters with little knowledge of the tradition and no interest in preserving anything other than a way to make money, but that criticism belongs in a later chapter.

Ron Hough meanwhile continues to work at Braunston, still painting roses and castles, although the boats are far more likely to be modern steel cruisers than carrying craft. With the huge number of pleasure boats now on the canal, Ron no longer needs to paint for the souvenir market, because an increasing number of discerning customers come to him for the final traditional flourish to their brand new boats. He now provides them, and us, with the only direct link back to the boat painters of the last century in an unbroken chain of teaching from father to son, from master to apprentice.

Ron Hough lettering a modern canal cruiser from the towpath near Braunston junction in July 1993.

COVENTRY
AND
POLESWORTH

A typical fantasy castle painting in 'Polesworth style' from the boatyard there operated by Lees and Atkins. This cabin block is the work of Jim Atkins.

Around 1840 Francis Sephton started or took a boat building business near Sutton Stop, where the Coventry Canal connects with the Oxford. It was clearly a prosperous concern, for by 1857 he had built a substantial public house as well, the Boat Inn, which in 1994 still remained under the control of a fifth generation Sephton descendant. Three of his sons followed him into the business, and even more grandsons. By the turn of the century they were running two yards at Hawkesbury, one on the Coventry right opposite the canal junction, and another at Tushes Bridge half-a-mile away on the Oxford Canal. At about the same time they sold yet another one at Polesworth, but it is not clear whether all three yards were operating simultaneously, or whether this sale was a re-grouping of their workforce in a more convenient place. The new owners at Polesworth went bankrupt quite quickly, so perhaps Sephton's took some of their customers with them.

The yards at Hawkesbury apparently continued to flourish into the 1920s, but there was an obvious and steady contraction of traffic during the depression and

both yards were closed during the 1930s, before the outbreak of World War II. Perhaps if they had still been in operation then, the extra work generated by the war may have carried them through to a different history. As it is they are a rather hazy memory for such an important business, with only a very few photographs surviving to tell their tale.

They did however build the *Friendship* for Joseph Skinner in 1924, the last horse-drawn boat to work on the Oxford Canal. That boat still survives as a museum exhibit at Ellesmere Port, a reminder of the life of one of the last owner-boatmen and of the skills of the Sephton boat builders; but *Friendship* has been repainted several times in her long life and no evidence of any original Sephton paintwork survives. Nor apparently does any exist elsewhere, in the experience of this author, although the surviving photographs clearly show richly decorated boats in the full traditional panoply of diamonds, roses and castles. None however are clear enough or close enough for us to distinguish or isolate the Sephton style from any other, or to identify any surviving objects as the work of that yard. This is a great pity, because they clearly must have had a significant influence in the area.

Luckily the same is not true of Lees and Atkins who took over the bankrupt yard at Polesworth, and who built up a very big reputation for their boat building, and especially for their boat decoration. It therefore became very popular with the owner boatmen of the area, and it may be that the firm developed its elaborate style of decoration precisely because it wanted to attract that important group of customers. The yard was in the heart of the coal mining country, but it was also in the centre of a whole clutch of boatyards servicing these coal boats, so competition and rivalry must have been intense. There were the two Sephton yards at Sutton Stop, Charity dock at Bedworth, William Nurser was

Some of the men at Sephton's boatyard at Longford aboard change boat Faith, *freshly docked and elaborately painted as an advertisement designed to appeal to their boating customers.*

Portrait of Mr Sephton of Sutton Stop.

not far away at Braunston, and there were soon to be two more yards at nearby Glascote, owned by two separate Barlows.

Henry Atkins (who, confusingly, was always called Harry) started the firm. He was born in 1869 and served his time in the 1880s at the Polesworth yard when it was in Sephton's ownership. When the new owners went bankrupt he went into partnership with his brother-in-law Harry Lees, who was a local butcher and baker, and they bought the business. Lees remained solely a financial partner, and it was Harry Atkins, clearly an astute businessman, who built boats and drove the company forward. It certainly seems to have prospered, for he eventually bought more land to extend the dock and several houses in the village as

well. By the evidence of an existing hire purchase agreement for a new boat called *Willie and Albert* for John Beech of Acton Bridge in 1913, the business was well established before World War I. They boasted a very distinguished letterheading which in turn proclaimed the ownership of a telephone, number 8 in Polesworth, and advertised themselves as dealers in lime and cement as well; this hints at a business relationship with Chas Nelson, the cement manufacturers, who were one of their boat-building customers. Things were going well.

Harry Atkins was the boss, the painter and signwriter, and the father of five sons, all of whom started work at the dock as they came of apprenticeship age. Henry, the eldest, began by taking over some of the decorative work, but an accident at the yard left him with a permanently damaged wrist. He could not continue boatbuilding and instead became the landlord of the local pub, the Royal Oak. The other four sons continued to work with their father, alongside a number of other workmen too, for there was a workforce of about twenty men when the yard was busy. Edward Crowshaw was one of them, yet another boat-builder, painter and signwriter, to be joined in 1924 by his son George, later to become an important painter at Braunston during the 1950s, as already mentioned in the preceding section. Len Shakespeare worked at Polesworth too, before becoming foreman and decorative painter at Samuel Barlow's new dock at Amington, near Tamworth, during the 1920s. All in all, Polesworth Dock was an important spot for the dissemination of the canal boat tradition.

Polesworth dockyard, believed to have been photographed when it was still owned by Sephton's, which would date this picture to the 1890s at least. The bowler-hatted signwriter working on the cabin of the day boat Jane is probably the yard foreman and could even be the owner, judging by the cut of his clothes.

The table-cupboard flap from the cabin of Thos. Clayton's motor boat Tay, *painted at Polesworth dock by Isaiah Atkins.*

James and Isaiah, who was the youngest son, became the specialist decorative painters, although Harry continued to do most of the signwriting on the boats until he retired. Both brothers painted in a very similar style learnt from their father, so similar that their flowers are almost indistinguishable from each other (even to Isaiah himself when shown examples in later life). Their castle scenes, however, developed an identifying individuality, although using much the same pictorial ingredients. A series of round towers with red and blue saucepan lid roofs, sprays of window slits and peculiar Moorish shaped doorways are characteristic of both, with a foreground pond edged with neat sprays of multi-coloured rushes; but the variations are more apparent in the paint handling than in the details of the imagery. Jim's paintwork generally appears to have been done at greater speed, to be less finicky than Isaiah's, also less considered and more intuitive and immediate, simply reflecting perhaps the confidence of the older brother. Isaiah's work in contrast is more careful and more self-conscious as an artist, and he continued to change and improve his painting style even as the carrying boat business contracted around him, for the decline was steady and must have been obvious throughout his working life.

The backbone of the business was work for the owner-boatmen, and they became fewer during the 1930s. New boats were built for Fellows, Morton & Clayton and Thos Clayton of Oldbury, but the only areas of real expansion were steel boats and motor boats and Lees and Atkins were not specialists in either of these fields. By the beginning of the war things were very tight and the work-force was basically down to the Atkins family. Harry was nearly seventy and decided to retire, and transferred the business to his four sons, but they still had

A typical 'Polesworth' style castle on the cabin side of John Wilson's motor boat Mabel in the 1940s, probably the work of Isaiah Atkins.

Another elaborately decorated boatyard-owned narrow boat, kept for customers to use whilst their own boat was on dock. This photograph was taken by E. Temple Thurston, and presumably dates from a time shortly before the publication of his book Flower of Gloster in 1911.

to diversify and take in outside jobs to survive. Then there was a sudden upsurge of work helping to maintain the Thos. Clayton tanker fleet, and as this was classed as work of national importance, Isaiah was recalled from the army to return to the boatyard at home again. Docking work for Clayton's, Cowburn and Cowpar, and the last few owner-boatmen kept the yard going into the 1950s but the end was becoming obvious. Daniel died in 1955, and with Jim approaching retirement age, the decision was made to wind up the boatyard business in 1959. Albert found a new job at the nearby colliery whilst Isaiah, by far the youngest of the brothers, continued working as a general carpenter for his son-in-law in the old premises until he too retired in 1975. Then for a while he was able at last to return to the boat painting that was really his first love. He died in 1989, rather saddened that the upsurge in interest in canals and traditional boatbuilding came a little too late to save Lees and Atkins famous boatyard from closure. Happily for us a considerable amount of his painted work survives in public and private collections as a memorial to one of the finest folk artists of the canals.

The Polesworth dock had a very high and well deserved reputation for its decorative paintwork, developed from the skills of a naturally talented family catering to the competitive demands of the owner-boatmen customers, whose main criteria for a good boat job, provided it did not leak, was that it should simply look better than anyone else's. The painter was given a surprisingly free hand to achieve that aim. Diamond patterns proliferated, with flowers and castles filling every available space, whilst extra decorative borders were added to the elaborately lettered name panels on the cabin side. A pair of crossed Union Jacks was sometimes painted on the cratch board. Isaiah remembered with pride a scene of horses jumping over a hedge that he painted on one particular deck board. Cigarette cards were used for reference material for dog's heads, and the

Six of the Atkins family and some of their men at Polesworth dock. Harry Atkins, the founder, is on the left and his youngest son Isaiah is the lad sitting at the front. As he was born in 1910 we can assume this picture dates from about 1925, shortly after Isaiah started work.

Player's sailor's head was painted on the handbowl. A reporter visiting the boat-yard in 1954 comments that as well as traditional castles, Isaiah also painted colourful renderings of Polesworth church, and Little Jim's cottage, a local historic feature of the neighbourhood, and he was always trying to vary his style of flowers. He was very impressed with the Hodgson style of rose painting on boats from the Stoke-on-Trent area, (see page 75) and kept the table flap from one of their cabins hung in the workshop as an example, and eventually developed his own individual version of that sort of cabbage rose. The more usual Polesworth flower, common to both Jim and Isaiah, and perhaps to Harry before them, is an open flower created with two or three pairs of opposing main brush strokes, with a mass of smaller strokes as much like stamens as petals enclosing the heart. All are painted with the under-painting still wet so that colours become brushed and blended together with some softness and subtlety. Who, one wonders, showed Harry the tricks of the trade in the 1880s? Atkins is a common name, but is it just coincidence that he shares it with Arthur Atkins, originally of Braunston, later of Hawkesbury, where he must certainly have known the Sephton family – or was Harry related to the many Atkins families working on the boats, some of whom became very talented painters? Are we beginning to get near the heart of the canal boat painting tradition, or should we be looking much further afield?

The Willie and Albert built by Lees and Atkins in 1915 for John Beech of Acton Bridge on the River Weaver. This photograph was taken in 1921, and records a very intricate paint scheme typical of the standards demanded by some of the owner-boatmen of the time, with masses of flowers on the rudder and top of the stern post as well as on the cabin side amongst the almost illegibly elaborate lettering.

MIDDLEWICH
AND
STOKE-ON-TRENT

'Knobsticks' was boatman's slang for the long established Anderton Company, the largest narrow boat carrier concentrating on traffic between the Staffordshire Potteries, Manchester, and the ports of Runcorn and Weston Point, where the Weaver meets the Mersey. Explanations of this nickname range from a nineteenth century word for a blackleg strike-breaker to the silver headed cane carried by the company's canal inspector who ranged the towpath, keeping a watchful eye on their boats and horses. Latterly the name became associated with pottery boats generally, and by association with the very distinctive style of decoration carried by many of them. The Anderton Company always had its own boat dock, originally at Anderton itself, but after 1912 at Middleport, whilst the second largest company in the area, the Mersey, Weaver & Ship Canal Carrying Company of 1894 had another boatyard nearby on the Burslem arm at Longport. Both companies had quite austere black-and-white colour schemes without fripperies; all additions in the roses and castles manner were paid for by the captain. The boats were well painted and maintained but relatively plain until after World War II when their attitude softened somewhat.

One of a pair of landscapes painted by Bill Hodgson in 1895 when he was 17. This one features the ruins of Tintern Abbey in the Wye valley and is probably worked up from a print or a photograph of this most popular sightseeing destination for those seeking the melancholic or the picturesque.

An elaborate group of typical Bill Hodgson's 'knobstick' style roses, painted as a display panel shortly before he retired in the late 1950s.

There were a host of more intricately decorated boats belonging to smaller companies right down to owner-boatmen with a single boat, and until the 1930s many of these independent smaller carriers used Tommy Williams' dock at Middlewich and Samuel Fox's dock at Westport in the Potteries. As traffic decreased and yards closed or merged so the boat work became more concentrated. When Fox's dock closed in the 1930s the remaining customers transferred their work to the Anderton Company dock at Middleport. When they were bought out by Mersey-Weavers in 1953 the new owners closed their own yard down and continued to use the better equipped 'knobstick' dock, and gave it an extra lease of life. Through all this contraction and change one man

A folding screen made and painted by Bill Hodgson in 1934 for use in the living room of his own house in Davenport Street.

continued his work as boat decorator and signwriter, and he was so prolific and his work was so popular with boatmen and bosses alike that his style has become synonymous with this whole corner of the narrow canal system.

William Henry Hodgson was born on 7 February 1878 in Crewe, but for some reason was brought up by his grandparents in Nantwich. He was small and dark and somewhat foreign looking, which he ascribed to a French grandmother, and he was something of an odd man out from the start. According to his wife he was spoilt as a child by his loving grandmother, which made him a rather autocratic and demanding husband and father in later life. He was very withdrawn and had something of a personality problem, but we are unlikely ever to know what caused or exacerbated a natural shyness towards excessive privacy. We have a very few paintings from his youth and a few snippets of family history to give us hints, but his wife has now been dead for a number of years, and his surviving children readily admit that they know little of his early life, for he preserved a very private personality even within his own family. His father was an engineering man in Crewe from an engineering background, and evidently intended his son for the same muscular career, for he brought the fourteen-year-old Bill back from his grandmother's house in Nantwich and entered him into an apprenticeship in the Crewe railway works. This was evidently not to his taste, for only

three years later he was painting scenery and pictures in London it is believed. He did some art school training in Birmingham at some point, but the details of this early career are very hazy. Luckily a few of his easel pictures survive from this period in the respectful care of his family, and it is from these pictorial statements that we have to deduce the stylistic development that was later to have such a large influence on northern narrow boat decoration.

Two of the pictures were painted in 1895 as a pair, and feature romantic views of the Wye valley, with hills and trees and water, and buildings in the middle distance in the standard landscape tradition, with some very strongly painted cattle in the foreground. One features the ruins of Tintern Abbey, whilst the other has a picturesque little black-and-white cottage nestling amongst the bushes, and both church and cottage were to recur in his cabin side paintings later on. Both these generalised subjects were already very popular in Victorian times, and remain calendar photograph favourites right up to the present day. Two slightly later paintings feature portrait figures, local worthies arguing village politics over the pub table in one, and an histrionic scene of three actors performing a dramatic moment in rich classical costume in the other – one of a pair of paintings from a show called 'The Sign of the Cross'. It is not clear whether any of these were original compositions, or were worked up from engravings, photographs or posters, but they do illustrate his painterly abilities at the time. Oddly enough he seems to do the difficult bits very well and the easy bits rather lazily. The faces are carefully painted with subtle pre-impressionist light and shade, the shape and texture of cloth is well observed and recreated, right down to a tiger skin rug on the stage floor, and his foreground cattle in the landscapes are particularly fine, but where one could expect a bit of slick theatrical technique to help, in the reflections in the water for example or feathery foliage in the trees, the painting is a bit clumsy. His understanding of perspective is a little sketchy, noticeable in some of his cabin side paintings much later on, which in turn suggests that his art school training was sketchy too, for perspective was one of the main thrusts of an academic art education of this time. But his handling of paint, colour and tone are lovely, and he was obviously an extremely talented young man, and one wonders what his future would have been if he had remained in the south and absorbed some of the freshness of the modern fine art movement of impressionism. Was there a sudden decision not to pursue a career as a fine artist but to concentrate on purely decorative applied art, or was there a gradual acceptance? Did he submit paintings to exhibitions and starve in a garret? Ten years later he was certainly back in Cheshire.

In 1908 William Hodgson married Jane Sweatman, the daughter of a Middlewich blacksmith, and he already described himself on his marriage certificate as a boat painter. His father-in-law set him up with a cottage and a large workshop above the smithy where amongst other jobs he painted scenery and backdrops for Crewe theatre. One of his local commissions was a pub sign for the King's Lock pub, and a portrait of a prize winning pigeon for the landlord, and this may have brought him to the attention of Tommy Williams, the boss of the boatyard next door, who in turn employed him to decorate canal boats for the first time.

It is not clear if he was employed at this dock full time, but his fame amongst the boat people spread from there, and a number of items of boat gear decorated by him when he was at Williams dock are still in existence, dating from the

W. H. Hodgson and his wife Jane in 1944.

The partner panel to the flowers illustrated on page 75. The central castle, swans, mountains and sunset colours are typical Hodgson boat painting, but the large tree and bunch of bulrushes are less common in his standard work.

time of World War I. Family mythology has it that the Middlewich boatyard did so well with Bill on the books that other yards were losing work, and Mr Samuel Fox finally came down from Westport to ask him to work for him. So keen was he that Mr Fox found the family a house in Davenport Street just over the railway line from the dock, and Bill Hodgson continued to work there until it closed in the 1930s. Then he transferred to the Anderton Company dockyard at Middleport, where he worked until he finally retired at seventy five years of age.

He was a quiet introverted man and yet he was an extroverted and obsessive painter, for painting was not just his job but his total way of life. How else can one account for the enormous amount of extra work he found time to do outside the long dockyard hours of boat painting? Money, or rather lack of it, was one pressure, for the boatyard pay was never great and he had a large family to support, as he and his wife reared eight children. He painted masses of cans and handbowls and cabin blocks privately in the back kitchen at home, for the boat people used to leave their equipment at the back door of his canalside house, and collect them newly painted a trip or two later. The garden was very often festooned with ropes of wooden bobbins from boat horse harness, being painted with colours and stripes.

Some Cheshire boatmen would act as an agent-cum-delivery service for the boating customers in the Runcorn area, taking new water cans up to him from the tinsmith at Preston Brook and bringing them downhill again when they were finished. This extra work was not just confined to boats, for he decorated furniture, fireplaces, mirrors and picture frames, and painted up the local ice cream van with a riot of pictures, roses and fancy lettering. He painted pictures on satin and velvet cushion covers, and made and painted a large three-leaf folding screen to sub-divide the small front room, smothering it in large confident paintings of colourful parrots and exotic birds. Then he announced, to the dread of the family, that he was going to paint the front room walls and ceiling as well. All they wanted was to blend into the locality as a nice unobtrusive ordinary potteries family, but paint it he did, with trees growing up the corners on to the ceiling with birds and bullrushes on the walls. It was successful, and the neighbours were invited to tea again with a very proud family, who no doubt were the talk of the neighbourhood for a while. Bill meanwhile carried on painting boats in his paint-stiffened old working coat.

Insofar as one can now recognise a 'mainstream' style of boat painting, it certainly seems that Bill was to one side of it to say the least. His flowers have always made a strong attempt at realism and a three-dimensional appearance compared to the great majority of canal painters, who were content to use and re-use a set pattern of brush strokes to create a floral design rather than a portrait of a real flower. But fifty years of boat painting inevitably led to a painting formula that could be whisked onto cupboards and handbowls with great speed, and one that was greatly admired and copied by the 'Cheshire' boatmen with varying degrees of success. He never gave up that old-fashioned desire for naturalism though; some of his very last pieces of work, done in semi-retirement for the small but growing group of pleasure boat enthusiasts around Stoke-on-Trent start to look more like gallery pieces than decorative applied art.

Several very talented boatmen-painters copied his style, but being boatmen first and painters in their spare time, they nearly all neaten up and simplify Bill's confident free-flowing brushwork into a slower more formal arrangement of brush strokes that is easier to copy and remember, and the results tend to be more naïve in effect.

A tunnel lamp decorated by Bill Hodgson at the Anderton Company dock.

Bill's castle and landscape pictures are immediately recognisable both by the atmosphere they evoke and the painting techniques employed. Considering his varied experience, and the fine quality of his picture painting, his boat work is a strange mixture of crude composition with polished technique, of unnecessarily heavy outlining over rich and subtle colour work. This is specially surprising when we know what he was capable of in his other work, even taking into account the ephemeral nature of boat work and the pressure from the boss to keep it cheap.

His castle panels nearly always place the building slap bang in the middle on a rounded hill with a symmetrical arrangement of mountains, lake, sailing boats and bushes on either side. The basic castle is a central round tower with the

*B*ill Hodgson *aboard John* Green's Duchess of York *outside the* Anderton Company's *slipway at Middleport.*

doorway in the middle, flanked by a tower either side with three black castle castellations on the top of each. On a wide narrow panel like a motor boat cabin block that is all you will get, but as the proportion of the space available allows more height, the castle grows another set of towers behind the first three, with tall red or blue spires, and the deeper foreground develops into a reed-fringed pond, perhaps bearing a pair of swans, which was another of Bill's trademarks. But the composition remains central and formal throughout, ignoring all the academic landscape teaching that we would have expected him to admire in the famous paintings of Claude, Turner and Constable. It also ignores the theatrical conventions that he must have been familiar with of massing bushes and trees on either side as foreground 'wings' to frame the middle ground of the architectural subject, to create depth and atmosphere. Instead he uses strongly contrasting tones within the building, blending from a pale ochery cream centre of each tower to a deep sienna brown shadow on both sides which, with a black outline, makes the castles stand out from his colourful sunset skies with gothic intensity. The background mountains are also blended to a very dark outline and these combined with the depth of colour and shadow he habitually painted into the bushes and their reflection in the lake, created a very personal and memorable mood, slightly reminiscent of the fashionable melancholia of Queen Victoria's widowhood, and the perfect material for popular taste.

In some ways Bill was perhaps a Victorian painter out of his time. It was his misfortune to be born at the very end of a period of decorative painting into a period of intense competition for what decorative work remained, as photography and the availability of ever cheaper coloured printing supplied the pictorial needs of the population. Luckily for us he found a surviving genre on the boats, and his wider artistic experience found expression in all the variations on the 'castle and roses' theme that his customers asked him to do. He painted birds,

dogs and horses on handbowls, working from pictures and cuttings he kept for reference for the boat people to choose from, and he painted the boatman's favourite – the sailor's head off the Player's packet – dozens if not hundreds of times. His landscapes inside the cabin on the walls could include farmhouses and churches as well as castles, and I was told of one occasion when he painted a picture of racehorses galloping past the winning post. His bunches of roses were painted on panels of colour to contrast with the oak graining; they were square or oval, surrounded by a filigree frame of brushstroke patterns, and sometimes complete with a painted string and nail to hang it on. As one boat-lady said, 'You didn't need any hanging plates in one of his cabins'.

Bill Hodgson died on 29 November 1957, disappointed perhaps that he had not achieved fame in the artistic world, although he would surely be pleased that his work is now so well remembered and respected by the boating population, old and new. He had worked almost full time up to the age of seventy-five when his work load was gradually taken over by Harold Hood, the dock foreman, who continued to paint in the Hodgson style, although without Bill's power and confidence. The days of the Anderton Company dock were already numbered however, and in 1958 the remaining couple of dozen Mersey-Weaver boats were absorbed into the North Western British Waterways fleet based in Northwich. Although the dockyard closed down soon afterwards, Bill Hodgson's style of painting lived on in the work of a number of boatmen-painters who were determined that 'Knobstick' style roses and castles should not be forgotten. They had become the proud regional badge of the Cheshire boatmen.

Mrs Clara Evans and her son Jimmy pose in the cabin doors of Snowflake *for a* News Chronicle *photographer in 1954.*

BANBURY
AND
LEIGHTON BUZZARD

The Tooley boatyard at Banbury has a very special place in any history of boat painting, for a number of reasons. It is as old as the canal, even older in one sense, for the dry dock was in use in 1778 before the southern link to Oxford was completed, and it has been in operation continuously ever since. At the time of writing it still survives, although successive waves of urban expansion and redevelopment have so altered it that it is difficult to remember how it was (and how it might have been). It is important as yet another example of a small

A beautifully decorated water can from the Oxford Canal, possibly painted by George Tooley of Banbury, or his son Herbert.

A panel painted by Herbert Tooley in the late 1940s for the cover of an Inland Waterways Association magazine. It was to be called 'The Cut', but the booklet never materialized, and this design and its companion panel for the front cover were never used.

boatyard whose main business was the maintenance of the boats of small independent carriers, the 'Number Ones' of the Oxford Canal. These were the men and women who, above all, demanded and maintained the most complex standards of painted decoration on their boats, and their demands comprise the nucleus of our subject.

It was also the boatyard at which *Cressy* was docked in 1939, the one to which the young philosopher engineer Lionel Rolt took his bride before setting out on his canal cruise which would eventually lead to the publication of *Narrow Boat*, with all the ramifications that followed. The atmosphere of Tooley's dock, and the values of the traditional craftsmanship that were exemplified there made an indelible impression on Rolt, and by recording and discussing those values in his book so persuasively, he affected much of the thinking of those that followed in his wake. There he watched old George Tooley at work ' . . . the battered bowler firmly planted on the back of his head, and a tray of many coloured paints at his elbow . . . the past miraculously living in the present'. Sadly, George died in 1940, but he passed his skills and the business on to his sons George and

Herbert, who maintained their father's standards and traditions into the 1980s. The boatyard eventually became the home as well as the workshop for Herbert Tooley, and its present survival is a memorial to a remarkable all-round craftsman, undoubtedly one of our finest canal painters and folk artists.

The boatyard side of the Tooley business began around 1900 when George rented the vacant dry dock and blacksmith's shop at Banbury from the Oxford Canal Company. His father Emmanuel was an owner-boatman, although from farming stock originally, mainly engaged in the carriage of steel and moulding sand from the Midlands to Banbury. George himself worked with his father for some time before deciding to take to boatbuilding at the age of thirty, apparently without any formal apprenticeship. Presumably he had gained some experience by maintaining his father's boats, and by watching other boatbuilders at work, and it would have been relatively easy, and certainly sensible, to employ a time served tradesman to help him set up the business. Certainly he would have known the needs of the boating customers from the inside, and had all the right contacts, and history seems to show that it was a very shrewd move. The yard became very busy in the period up to World War I and employed a couple more boatbuilders; Emmanuel stopped boating and came to work for his son. They kept the boats, however, partly carrying and partly as hire or 'change' boats for their customers to use whilst their own boats were on dock. The business was mainly concerned with repair work, but they did build a dozen new boats over the years, mainly to have plenty of work on hand to keep employed in the slack periods between jobs. But the firm's prosperity was very intimately linked with that of their boating customers, and the years of slump and depression hit very hard. Things picked up during the war years, but the Number Ones and canal carrying by horse boat died away very quickly after the war and another lean period ensued. This time however the expanding pleasure boat business began to fill the gap, offering a new lease of life for Tooley's boat yard.

The style of paintwork now associated with the Tooleys may once more owe its ancestry to the Nursers. Ernest Carvell was a boatbuilder from Braunston who was employed by old George to work at Banbury in the early days partly because,

'Painting the can' – a scraperboard illustration by D. J. Watkins-Pitchford for L. T. C. Rolt's Narrow Boat published in 1944, and based on 'a photograph of George Tooley taken by Angela Rolt.

Herbert Tooley (nearest the camera) and his brother George surveying a boat in the dry dock at Banbury.

according to Herbert, he was adept at painting roses and castles. He finished work at the Tooley's yard around 1927 just as Herbert, who was born in 1913, left school and started full-time work at the yard. From that time onwards it was George Tooley senior who did most of the decoration necessary, having learned to do it himself by watching Carvell at work. He was clearly a very naturally gifted all-round craftsman to be able to absorb and practise these new skills well after most tradesmen had stopped learning, and his two sons followed in his footsteps. George Tooley junior, the elder brother by ten years, concentrated on the signwriting side of the decorative work, and having worked alongside Ernest Carvell may have learned from him, although another local signwriter, a Mr Hitchman, was also employed occasionally who may have influenced his style as well. Herbert meanwhile concentrated on the roses and castles and the cabin graining, developing his father's style into the much respected personal trademark of the Banbury boatyard. Both brothers were primarily boat builders, spending most of their time working with heavy oak and elm planks and iron knees, which makes the delicacy and gentleness of their painted work all the more remarkable.

During the 1950s Joe Skinner's *Friendship*, the last horse-drawn carrying boat to operate on the Oxford Canal was docked at the Banbury boatyard and the cabin was entirely repainted inside and out. This boat and cabin survive as a museum exhibit at the Boat Museum at Ellesmere Port, and the interior of the cabin still carries all the elaborate graining and painting work of Herbert Tooley in his prime, a perfect reminder of the conjunction between canal life, work and folk art that is the central obsession of this book. It is grained throughout in two contrasting shades of colour, mahogany for the beams, the side bed and the cabin side panel framing, with a rich orangey light oak graining for everything else. Mouldings are picked out in yellow and red, and the panels are outlined again with extra painted borders in green or blue, with fancy corner designs. Every available panel and cupboard door is decorated with a castle picture or a bunch of roses, some on a contrasting green oval panel with their own brown brush-stroke border pattern, before each individual panel is finished off with a little scroll design or elaborate *fleur-de-lis* in each corner.

It is a remarkable and unique exhibit, and provides a wonderful catalogue of Herbert Tooley's style of painting in one place, his subtle friendly flowers set in a neat arrangement of leaves and his multi-towered castles, with each landscape composition noticeably different from the next. The ingredients are personal and relatively limited, but each picture is a bold re-arrangement of the Tooley elements, the towers and turrets with neatly painted stonework patterns, the flat arched bridges all set against a pink sunset sky. Trees are noticeable by their absence, but each area of the castle grounds or foreground fields is blended to a darker edge like a hedge, with greeny-yellow highlights worked into the wet paint with a stiff brush. It is when he chooses to include square towers or flat walls that his limitations as a naturalistic painter are most exposed, for like most canal boat painters, his understanding of perspective is poor and these paintings are more noticeably 'wrong'.

Observers' attitudes to this lack of sophistication vary widely. To some it is simply childish ignorance which a little hard work would eradicate, whilst to others it is charming *naïveté*, by-passing artistic inhibitions, and expressing a greater universal truth. As the reader will probably have deduced, this author inclines toward the latter belief, and the work of Herbert Tooley of Banbury seems to me to be a masterly balance between commercial decoration and lovely unsophisticated art. This shy and retiring craftsman and folk artist continued to work at his famous dockyard until his death in 1987.

Portrait of a master painter of the canals – Frank Jones at work on a converted pontoon Wagtail *at Linslade.*

A metal tray decorated in typical flamboyant style by Frank Jones of Leighton Buzzard.

A castle panel painted by William Allen sometime before 1930, and treasured within his family ever since.

The art of Frank Jones of Leighton Buzzard provides an interesting contrast to Herbert's work. Frank too was primarily a boat builder, but quite early in his career he chose to specialise towards the paintwork and his more constant practice as well as his personality produced paintings with a very different atmosphere. The colours are sharp, the background landscapes to his rather oriental looking castles are more expansive and the atmosphere is brighter and more forceful. His flowers are bigger and more variegated and expand to fill the available space compared to Herbert's more tentative bunches which just occupy the central space, whilst Frank's brush-work is clearly faster and full of self confidence. He is especially interesting to the later history of boat painting not just because he was such an excellent painter, but because he became so well known, and something of a media star. Not only was he well placed geographically on the canal, on the busy London to Birmingham route where standards were high and boating lasted longest, but he was also near a railway station conveniently near London. When a comment was required from the working craftsman's point of view, or a press photograph was needed of folk art in action, Frank seemed happy to oblige.

At the end of World War II, journalists, like gardeners searching out new shoots in the spring, saw in the survival of the boat painting craft a nostalgic hope for a return to pre-war normality, for the survival of colourful old-time craftsmanship and values. Here in Frank Jones was living proof. He and his work were regularly featured in magazines and newspapers, he was interviewed on the radio in 1947 and 1949, he gave public demonstrations at the first Inland Waterways Association rally at Market Harborough in 1950, appeared on television in 1953, and on the radio again in 1955. His celebrity status was clearly to his liking; he had business cards specially printed describing himself simply as an 'Artist Decorator'.

Frank was born in Hemel Hempstead in 1904 but he and his brother were brought up by their stepmother in Rickmansworth. Anthony Walker's book

A small water can or milk can decorated by William Allen with a style of flower quite different to the more usual style of canal roses, and one that re-appeared in the work of his pupil, Frank Jones, much later on.

about his family's boatyard says that Frank started his apprenticeship there, but he does not seem to have completed a full seven years, for when he was nineteen years old he moved and started work at Faulkner's dock at Leighton Buzzard. It is there that Frank Jones himself said that he learned his painting trade, under the tutelage of the master boat builder William Allen. In fact he lodged with Billy Allen and his wife for several years before he married a local girl and set up his own home in Edward Street, and it is to Mr Allen that we must look for a significant influence on Frank's life and work.

Billy Allen's grandchildren relate as family history that he had previously worked at Berkhamsted, presumably at the Costin's boatyard which closed in 1910. Therefore it seems a reasonable supposition that he moved to Linslade then, to work for Lawrence Faulkner who had previously been one of Costin's customers, and who had set up his own repair facilities at Leighton Buzzard. Perhaps the Jones and Allen families were already acquainted when Frank was still a child at Hemel Hempstead, for it would otherwise seem to be an unusually close working relationship that would involve an employer taking an apprentice in as a lodger as well. Billy Allen was born in 1861, and when he was married in Heyford in Northamptonshire in 1883 his job was entered as a boatbuilder and labourer. This must surely point to an apprenticeship and courtship in that area, close to Thompson's boatyard at Nether Heyford, and only a few miles from William Nurser's yard at Braunston. One more thread of evidence seems to lead back to this important junction. Then he worked at Willesden for a while, then at Berkhamsted before finally settling in Linslade where he remained until his death in 1934.

His talents and his situation as an unusual or exceptional craftsman were clearly recognised by somebody outside the canal world, because a fading press cutting from *The Daily Sketch* shows him posing 'with some of the work he is showing at the exhibition of bargee-art in Marylebone-Lane'. It is unfortunately undated, and as yet untraced, but it shows him as an elderly man and therefore probably dates from the late 1920s or early 1930s. This was the man who was Frank's mentor, and whose mantle he inherited when Billy Allen retired. Perhaps it is less surprising that after this early brush with celebrity, Frank had a heightened sense of the importance of his art and craft in the wider world, at least in comparison to the reticence shown by such men as the Tooley's.

Frank Jones' employer for most of his working life was L. B. Faulkner who operated a fleet of well decorated narrow boats mainly carrying sand from the Leighton Buzzard area to London and Birmingham, and who ran his own boat-yard to service these boats from about 1910. At its peak capacity Faulkners' had over fifty boats working, but the fleet was much reduced by the time Lawrence Faulkner died in 1950, and the business was closed. The boatyard at Charity Wharf, Linslade, was bought by a local coach building and car company, Camden Motors, which continued to operate it as a general repair yard with Frank as the foreman manager. In 1956 it was finally decided to close the boat-yard, but Frank continued to work for Camden Motors as a coachbuilder, for motor bodies and lorry cabs still required a great deal of skilled carpentry at that period.

It was not the end of his boat painting career however, for he had a wide reputation and considerable personal pride in his work. He continued to paint at home as a hobby, painting trays, firescreens, and crinoline ladies on mirrors as

well as traditional items for the working boatmen, and an increasing number of pleasure boat owners searched him out and asked him to paint cans and stools for them too. Ever since then his work has been respected and collected and is satisfyingly well represented in several collections both public and private. A post-war cutting from the local newspaper quotes him as having already had some of his work exhibited in London and America, and Faulkner, who was clearly a fan of his employee, lent several items painted by Frank to the touring IWA exhibition in 1947. At about the same period he painted a whole range of boat equipment for the British Council, for an exhibition of English Popular Art that toured Australia and New Zealand, and when that returned it became part of the Museum of English Rural Life's collection, and is now on display at Blakes Lock, Reading.

It is a fine and fitting tribute to a man who, although he became quite famous in his own right, never sought to promote himself as anything more than part of an honourable tradition of boatmen and decorative painting; as he said in a radio interview in 1949 '. . . The shape of my roses would be my own idea, but in general I followed on the style of the old painter who taught me and he'd followed on from someone else before'. It was a disappointment to him, and a great loss to us, that he never managed to find a proper apprentice to carry on his trade in the traditional way for ' . . . you don't seem to get young fellows with the patience for this sort of thing . . . it's a terribly cold job sitting painting on a boat'. But when Frank Jones died in 1970 at the age of sixty-six he personally had already done a great deal to ensure that the canal boat traditions would not be forgotten in the near future.

*F*rank Jones with some of his *work aboard one of L. B. Faulkner's boats at Leighton Buzzard.*

RICKMANSWORTH
AND
TRING

H arry Walker started a new boatyard in Rickmansworth in 1905 and it progressed very fast and successfully. W. E. Costin's yard at Berkhamsted, successors to Peacock & Willett's who started the boatyard soon after the canal

A water can painted by Frank Jones which, with this castle inside the lid, must surely have been a display piece for one of the many exhibitions in which his work was featured in the 1950s.

opened in 1798, closed the boatbuilding side of their business in 1910, and one cannot but wonder whether the two events were connected in some way. Both were servicing boats working the Grand Junction Canal, and if the one could expand so successfully, surely the other could be expected to at least survive. Their third competitor for the market, Bushell Bros. at Tring, weathered the storm well.

The boats for this part of the canal system were a mixture of narrow boats that could work anywhere on the canal system and wide boats which were confined to the Grand Junction Canal, Regent's Canal and to some degree to the River Thames. The Grand Junction was nominally a barge canal, able to accommodate 14-foot (4 metres) beam craft all the way to Braunston, but in practise these maximum sized barges only usually worked as far north as Harefield, and occasionally to Berkhamsted. Beyond that the canal itself was of such a small cross-section that it was often difficult for two such craft to pass each other and wide boat traffic was confined to boats that varied from 9 to 12 feet (3 to 4 metres) wide, built like curved sided narrow boats. Even then the tunnels at Braunston and Blisworth were a problem because they were not big enough to allow these wide up-country boats to pass an ordinary narrow boat. One-way traffic and consequent delays were the unpopular result. In practice very few of these wide boats went further north than the sand quarries at Leighton Buzzard, but from there to London they were an important proportion of the commercial craft. They are not narrow boats in the usual sense of the expression, but they were constructed like narrow boats, had a similar sort of stern cabin and clothing-up arrangement, and were very often worked by families who lived on them in cabins considerably more spacious than an ordinary narrow boat could offer. They also carried the same traditional painted decorations of roses and castles and thus fall firmly within the scope of this book.

Sometime in the 1850s John Bushell started repairing some of the boats that supplied Meade's flour mills at Tring alongside the Wendover Arm, and by 1875 this had developed into a thriving independent business, run by his son Joseph, on a piece of ground rented from the mill. In about 1895 William Henry Walker (but known to his family as Harry) started an apprenticeship at the Bushell boatyard to learn the trade. Ten years later this confident young man signed an agreement with Lord Ebury to lease Frogmore wharf in Rickmansworth, and he started up in opposition to Bushell. His late employer must have viewed his young protégé's meteoric business success with mixed feelings. So too must Costin's of Berkhamsted, for it was with two of their boatbuilders, John Gould and Fred Collyer, that Harry started the business.

In terms of experience and useful contacts in the canal world he was very well placed, for his father had by this time been a section inspector and overseer for the Grand Junction Canal for twenty years, and was personally in an influential position to forcefully suggest that his son's new business needed clients. Perhaps he supplied financial backing too, for Harry launched his enterprise on several linked business fronts: he was a timber dealer, a coal and coke merchant and a supplier of builders materials, and many of these goods were delivered in his own boats, built and maintained at his own boatyard. It was a very good balanced portfolio and it progressed well. At the end of 1905 this young man of twenty-four was already employing twenty-five men. His younger brothers, Percy and Sidney, joined him in the business and it was as W. H. Walker & Brothers Ltd

A boat horse nose tin decorated at Bushell Bros dock at New Mills near Tring, probably the work of Alf Fenemore, but possibly a copy of his work by Charlie Bushell done in his retirement.

George Baxter at work in 1939 at Walker's dock at Rickmansworth, decorating a pair of boats belonging to one of the decreasing number of owner-boatmen on the Grand Union Canal at the time.

that they traded successfully until the ground was sold for redevelopment in 1988. The history of this company has been thoroughly documented in *Walkers' of Ricky*, written by Harry's nephew Anthony Walker, and this present book wishes to acknowledge a great debt to his careful work.

Considering how many excellent quality photographs survive from the early days, and how complete are the dock records, the lack of reliable information about their decorative painters is surprising, and frustrating. Like the Sephton's evidence, the photographs clearly show Walker's boats very neatly and thoroughly decorated with diamonds, and roses and castles on the doors, but none were taken quite near enough to the boats to be able to distinguish the style or quality of the artist's work, and no names come down to us. It does serve as a timely reminder, however, that boat decorators were not in general offered any particular respect as specialists or artists; they were simply carrying out part of their trade as canal boatbuilders. Maybe Harry himself did some of the early boats in a style learnt at Bushell Bros. dock, or perhaps it was one of the ex-Costin's boatbuilders who might have worked with Billy Allen. Walter Gent was foreman of the dock in the early 1930s, and as he had transferred from Faulkner's yard in Leighton Buzzard he would almost certainly have come into contact with Mr Allen. Frank Jones worked there for a while around 1920 when he was a very young apprentice before himself transferring to Faulker's, and he might have started painting by doing some of Walker's boats under the eye of an older man.

In 1934 Walker Brothers boatyard began building new narrow boats for the new Grand Union Canal Carrying Company at an escalating rate, four at the end of 1934, twenty-two in 1935 and a staggering forty-six in 1936, all at a time when other yards were closing down for lack of work. It is true that Walker's had

developed considerable expertise with motor boats from their earliest days, but it was their readiness to adjust their premises and their workforce to the demands of the expanding GUCC Co. that helped them to gain these most useful contracts. Paradoxically, this busiest of all periods saw the least decorative paintwork produced at Walker's, for it was the declared intention of the new company to design a less elaborate livery for their boats than was normal or traditional in order to promote their progressive modern image. All that was specified was the simplest paintwork with clear straightforward lettering, and a local signwriter from Rickmansworth was contracted to letter the boats as they were finished. His name was Bert Barr, and he must have been delighted, for Walker's were completing two a week at the very peak of production. He continued this business relationship with Walker's after the completion of this big order in 1938. Initially he only did the lettering, and to a very high professional standard, according to a couple of the boatbuilders who worked there at the time. But in the period following the war he took up the roses and castles side of the work

Wide boat Langley designed and built to work on the Grand Junction Canal carrying grain for Toovey's mill. The 'Built by Bushell Bros' signboard set up for the photograph suggests that this picture records her appearance on launching day in 1916.

The butty Albert tied alongside the Yarwood-built motorboat Victoria at Bushell Bros yard, perhaps soon after they built and launched her in 1931 for Associated Canal Carriers Ltd, the forerunner of the Grand Union Canal Carrying Co.

A corner of Charlie Bushell's workshop at his home at New Mills in 1960, packed with canal memorabilia, tools, boat equipment, and items of painted ware from the boatyard which had closed in 1952.

as well, and became effectively the regular dock decorator, although not employed directly by Walker Brothers.

By the 1950s canal carrying was clearly coming to an end, and although Walker's were accommodating sufficient pleasure boat work to keep the remaining boatbuilders employed, the decision was taken to expand the more profitable building and fencing side of the business instead. The boat repair facility was finally closed in 1964, after being an honourable part of canal history for nearly sixty years. Twenty-five years later the site became a supermarket.

Joseph Bushell's boatyard on the Wendover Arm, at which Harry served his apprenticeship, seems to have survived the Walker Brothers competition very well, and his sons Joseph and Charlie joined their father in the business, and continued to trade as Bushell Brothers when he retired in 1912. It was a relatively small yard, with only one boat's length of slipway, although two or three craft could be built or worked on side by side. It progressed from an entirely open piece of ground with no buildings except a blacksmith's shop to, eventually, a fully covered slipway with a range of well-equipped workshops. They built fishing punts, narrow boats, Grand Junction style wide boats, bigger barges for the Regent's Canal and an enormous tug that only just squeezed through the locks and under the bridges on her way to London, to be finished off on the Thames. They had in addition a wheelwright's shop and a coachbuilding department working on road vehicles, and this diversity and flexibility kept the business running until the brothers decided to retire in 1952. The site was then reclaimed by the flour mill next door, now owned by Heygates, who have expanded their premises over the old boatyard area.

In the last years of its life the decorative paintwork was handled by Alf Fenemore, a local man who worked at Bushell's for most of his life and where he presumably learnt his trade. Of the two Bushell brothers Joseph, the office partner, was possibly the more artistic one, although it was Charlie who took up boat painting as a hobby after he retired. It is not known whether their father, Joseph Bushell senior, painted the boats, but an oil painting by him of horses ploughing a field remains in the family and proves that he was a capable amateur artist.

The well-provenanced boat painting work that survives from Bushell Bros dock seen by this author is something of a puzzle, for much of it came from Charlie Bushell's garden workshop years after he retired and it is not now clear whether this is the work of Alf Fenemore, or Charlie copying Alf's work as a hobby, which he certainly did. There are two handbowls, a horse's nose tin, stool, water can, headlamp, cabin block and several small tin panels with castles painted on them as decorative plaques, all clearly painted by the same hand. The castles have a naïve charm and simplicity, but the flowers seem surprisingly graceless and lumpy for a professional. The roses are large with thick finger-like petal strokes with little sense of form underlying the brushstroke pattern, the smaller pansy-type flowers look a little like whirling swastikas, whilst the leaves eddy around them in a rather unsettling way. In contrast, the castle pictures seem calm and delicate. The building is centred on a round tower whose top is slotted with one or two massive castellations, topped with a tri-coloured flag streaming off to the right. The tower is flanked by a couple of other buildings, whilst a pitched roofed building in front acts as gatehouse, with a curved path or drive sweeping down to the right. Most noticeable however is its relationship to a bridge, one or two arches spanning a river on the left, neatly marked all over with a strong stone-work pattern. Each landscape is finished off with much fencing drawn on in black, but with little sense of perspective. These castle pictures are charming, but they lack the dash and flair that one usually associates with a dockyard painter's work, and further comment should perhaps await further evidence. This is a pity as photographs of Bushell Bros boats show them lavishly decorated, and it would be good to name an individual or two.

A castle painting on the top of a cabin stool made and painted at Bushell Bros. dockyard, probably the work of Alfie Fenemore.

Fellows, Morton & Clayton Ltd were one of the largest companies to operate narrow boats on the canals, and were probably the best known. This is part-ly because they built up a country-wide canal carrying service, and their boats became a familiar sight in many centres of industry and population, in Birmingham, Wolverhampton, Nottingham, Leicester, Manchester and London, as well as everywhere in between. They also had a very long history, for even when the FM&C name was officially incorporated in 1889, some of the constituent parts of the amalgamation had been operating for over forty years.

FM&C were a progressive company however, and amongst the earliest users of steam and diesel power to drive narrow boats. They were successful and efficient, and although not known for being over generous, they earned the loyalty and respect of their boat crews over several generations. The company in turn appeared to respect the painting traditions of the boat people for, whilst not being elaborately decorated compared to the boats of some of the smaller com-panies, the cabin doors and table cupboard in the cabin were always painted with roses and castles at the expense of the company. The cost of any further decoration in the cabin was paid for by the captain, as was common with other

A table-cupboard and a pair of cabin doors painted by George Preston, photographed at Yarwood's dockyard on the River Weaver where many FM&C motor boats were built in the 1930s.

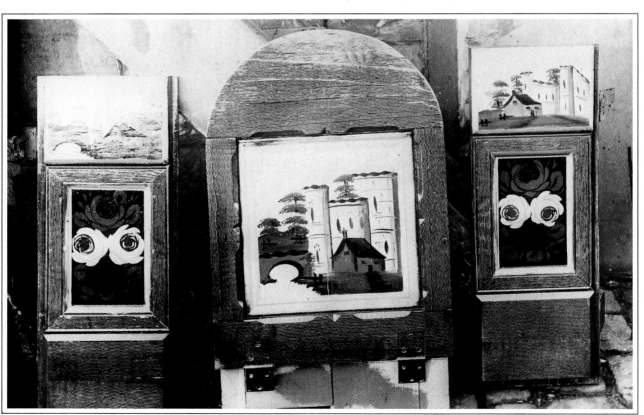

carriers. The outside paintwork was plain but smart, with bold lettering and scrolls filling the cabin side panels. The company livery was originally black-and-white with a touch of red, similar to their main competitors on the northern narrow canals, the Anderton Company and the Shropshire Union Carrying Company, but in the 1920s the colour scheme changed to a more cheerful red, yellow and green. Because of their fame and importance, FM&C's attitude to their crews, their painting, and their painters is especially important to us.

They had two boatyards of their own but also contracted work out to several other docks. Boats were built for them by Lees and Atkins and by Sephtons for example, and many of the new motor boats built in the 1920s and 1930s came from the shipyard of W. J. Yarwoods in Northwich, but much of their building and repair work was carried out in house. The expanded company acquired a small boatyard at Saltley in Birmingham when it absorbed William Clayton's business in 1889, and in 1895 it undertook a substantial expansion there. This Birmingham boatyard came to specialise in the iron boats in the fleet, whilst the other yard at Uxbridge remained almost exclusively concerned with the wooden boats. This had previously belonged to Edward Morgan and was taken over in 1896. Both yards must have had several painters in their history but only three names have been firmly recorded as decorative painters, and all from the last few years of independent existence just prior to nationalisation in 1948.

In Birmingham it was George Preston who was the specialist. He was born in 1875, and if he started work at the usual age of fourteen his lifetime's work almost exactly matches that of his employer, for he died in 1949. It is not clear whether he started out as a general boatbuilder, or as a painter, but by the 1930s he was certainly a respected specialist signwriter and decorator. He was dispatched by train to Northwich to add the final touches to FM&C's new boats at Yarwoods, but his services were employed by Yarwoods on boats for other carrying companies too, for Cowburn & Cowpar and Associated Canal Carriers. Thanks to their company policy of carefully documenting their work with photographs, we have one picture that clearly identifies the Preston style of rose and castle at this date. With this evidence, other views of boat painting can be identified with reasonable confidence as having been painted by George Preston.

In Uxbridge the decoration was done by Henry Penn, or Harry Crook, or both. Harry Crook was the dock foreman at Uxbridge when the yard, along with the company, became part of the nationalised Docks & Inland Waterways executive in 1948, and his name has been suggested to me as the main decorative painter; but Mr Penn is mentioned and quoted by name in *Canals Barges and People* by John O'Connor in 1950. This book describes '. . . the more formal flowers of Uxbridge . . . two or three roses depicted back to back as if painted against a mirror' contrasted with '. . . the loose type of rose painting from Braunston'. This contrast is confirmed by the many examples of Uxbridge painting which survive, for they are tight ball-like flowers built up very symmetrically on a neat crescent whose points almost meet, surrounded by a necklace of fat teardrop petal shapes. They are attractive, but far from flamboyant, and in their abstract formality they are closer to a lot of the flowers of international folk art. Preston's flowers are built on an equally rigid formula, although larger and more confident, which suggests they stem from the same source. A much earlier reference in *By Shank and Crank* by Edmund Vale in 1924 also comments on the simplicity of the Uxbridge paintwork compared to the other school of artistry 'florid

G eorge Preston *(1875–1949), the signwriter and boat decorator at Fellows, Morton & Clayton's dock at Saltley in Birmingham.*

*M*otor boat Edward *with paintwork by George Preston, photographed at Yarwoods dockyard in 1932.*

to an excess'. No name is given to the master painter interviewed but he 'belonged to the simple school, and I could not but think that the effects he achieved were very much finer than those of the florid craftsman. He treated his rudders and tillers with broad bands of colour in place of bunches of grapes and posies . . .'. Was this good taste or penny-pinching? Aesthetics or incompetence? 'But in his panels . . . he let himself go a little. His favourite device was a splendid chateau-mansion in warm browns wrought in a curious convention of perspective, with a simultaneous marine and mountain background, in the middle distance of which sails or swans were always in evidence.'

In the 1940s the Uxbridge style castle had simplified still further to three or four very straight thin round towers on the right of the picture, painted in contrasting yellows and browns, each surmounted by a flagpole carrying a red pennant. Mountains in the background and the field in the foreground are skimpy in the extreme. George Preston's castles too are clearly painted to a fast formula with no unnecessary additional material, and one wonders whether the Fellows, Morton & Clayton painters were actually conforming to a company policy to save costs. Perhaps the company would have liked to do away with it altogether, and merely paid for the minimum amount of decoration to keep their boat people loyal to them. As the foreman boatbuilder at Uxbridge ruefully commented to Edmund Vale in the early 1920s 'if the colour's all right, the boat don't leak'.

In the amalgamation of 1889 the company of Fellows & Morton, which dated from 1876, was combined with that of William Clayton which had been trading since 1842. By then Clayton's was under the management of William's son Thomas who decided to keep the bulk liquid carrying side of the business as a separate concern, so he moved his centre of operation to Oldbury and ran a fleet of narrow boat tankers as Thos Clayton (Oldbury) Ltd. This new company maintained close connections with FM&C, for Thomas was made a managing director of the new concern as well, and much of his boatbuilding and repair work was carried out at the docks at Uxbridge and Saltley. As both companies expanded however, work had to be increasingly contracted out to other boatyards, but it was not until 1935 that Thos Clayton's finally decided that they needed to run their own repair yard. They set up a boatyard on a new site near their office and stables in Oldbury, close to the junction with the Titford branch, and continued to maintain the fleet there until traffic ceased in 1966. From a comparatively late entry into the business it remained to become one of the last canal boatyards to survive solely on commercial traffic.

Fred Winnet worked there throughout its existence. Born in 1902, he had served his boatbuilding apprenticeship at Chance & Hunt's dock at Oldbury, a company that also ran bulk liquid carriers, before he moved to Braunston to work at Nurser's boatyard for five years, where many of Clayton's tankers were built. Prior to Clayton's opening their own slipway Fred was working in Oldbury again, at Hale's dock, another of the firms that built new boats for Thos. Clayton over the years, and one of their regular maintenance yards. He was clearly an ideal man for the new yard, fully experienced, a good craftsman and by this time a good painter too. He was already signwriting and lettering boats at Hale's yard,

(Above)
A cabin door decorated at the Fellows Morton & Clayton dock at Uxbridge. This is either the work of Harry Crook or Henry Penn, and being a fairly simple style, with each flower built up from a neat crescent with surrounding teardrop petals, it is the basic pattern copied by many painters.

◆◆

A seatboard decorated by Fred Winnett in about 1960 with his characteristic formalised flower pattern, the painted trademark of the Thos. Clayton dock at Oldbury.

◆◆

Boat captain Danny Jinks and his family aboard Dane *and* Gipping *tied up at Oldbury.*

but at Clayton's, under the new foreman, Joey Monk, Fred became the specialist painter and signwriter throughout the dock's existence. He ended up as the dock foreman as well.

Fred developed what can most politely be called a very odd style of flower painting, one that seems to offer very little allegience to any other existing boat painting. It is interesting, and does the job of filling the door panels and the spaces between the lettering with a neat decorative pattern adequately, but his flower painting became so formalised and stylised that what resulted was an abstract pattern making technique with little sense of natural growth or grace. Nevertheless these 'Clayton Cabbages' became the trademark badge of the yard and company, an interesting development at the edge of the boat painting tradition.

Each main flower has a central cup shape enclosed by a pair of long petal strokes reaching around it, with three little semicircular shaped petals at the leading edge. Secondary colours are then dragged in with a crude dry-brush technique, but the decorative quality of these flower groups relies more strongly than usual on the leaf pattern behind them. The leaves are painted very precisely and identically, neat green ovals, each with a semicircular dark shadow emerging from behind the flowers. The outermost tips of the leaves are picked out with strong white highlights, and when these are linked by two curved dashes of yellow neatly placed between each leaf, each flower group becomes surrounded by a chain of curves that acts as a decorative border. The pattern making became far more important than any idea of flower painting.

Fred's cabin door castles are not very attractive either. They are invariably built up with three towers, the central one slightly higher than the others, with a curtain wall sweeping up on either side with no attempt at realism. The buildings are painted in a flat dirty yellow brown with details and an outline drawn on in thin black lines, and they squat centrally like a child's version of a medieval fortress. This lack of artistry, or of professional flair, is surprising when it is considered how

many boats Thos Clayton's were running, just how much practice Fred must have had over the years, and how many examples of other painters' work were already present in the fleet to set a standard. The quality of Clayton's paintwork was excellent in other respects, for Fred was a very good craftsman, but he did not seem to have the same latent artistic talent that so many other boatbuilders apparently had, waiting to be released through boat painting conventions.

One of the men working under Freddie Winnet at Oldbury was Billy Birch, and he too could decorate a boat quite adequately, painting in that same style that had become peculiar to Clayton's dock, although he was primarily a carpenter-boatbuilder. In 1954 they took on a new young apprentice to learn the trade as well, William Blunn, the youngest child of one of the Clayton's boating families, and possibly the last lad to enter the trade with a genuine expectation of working on commercial wooden narrow boats as a major part of his work. Unfortunately he was to be disappointed, for as he progressed through his training the canal carrying businesses were contracting around him. From Olbury he went to work at Braunston for a year, but there too the end of canal carrying was in sight, and with regret he went to work as a general carpenter on the land. It was nearly thirty years before he returned to boatbuilding work on the canal again, but throughout that period he still continued to paint roses and castles as a hobby. Now he provides us with one of the very few direct links with the world of traditional canal boatbuilding, and the old master to apprentice system.

*T*hos Clayton butty Erne *at work, with a young crew experiencing the less romantic aspects of family boating, in the snow.*

CHAPTER 5

BOATMEN-PAINTERS

A *can and a hand bowl*
painted in two variations
of the boatman's 'Knobstick'
style, developed from the work
of Bill Hodgson of the
Anderton Company dock.
Water can by Reg Barnett,
hand bowl by George Wain.

Hand bowl decorated by Reg Barnett in his typical neat and tight 'Knobstick' style. His castles, whilst including a number of Hodgson elements, were generally made more interesting by being moved off centre and including some extra features like the Russian-style onion dome shown here.

The majority of canal boat art was from the professional hands of boat-builders and painters who decorated the boats as part of their job, but there was a smaller, but equally important proportion done by the boat population themselves. It is logical to call it amateur work as distinct from the commercially paid work from the boatyards, but the slightly perjorative sense that the word 'amateur' suggests does not do justice to the personal involvement that the boat people felt for their own special art, nor for the importance that it had within their community. It was just one of the layers of tradition that the boat people clothed themselves in so as to stand apart from the land population. It was a statement of separateness, yet one so attractive that it is difficult to criticise as smug or exclusive. The profusion of flowers and pictures was always unusual – extra-ordinary perhaps, certainly unnecessary, but never ugly or hurtful; they damaged nothing and nobody, a simple pleasure to the eyes of the onlooker, whether canal worker or not. The paintings were a positive visual statement

about an attitude to home and work, and from the boatman's point of view they were very useful, for they countered some of the usual assumptions about 'common bargees' – the accusations of slovenliness and dirt. So painting roses and castles became an important spare time occupation for many boatmen.

The overall appearance of the boat could be seen as a guide to the quality of the boatman and his family. A clean well painted boat suggests a clean well scrubbed family within, with a careful and conscientious captain who would serve an employer well. Any sensible employer will seek to keep such a captain contented, and if that man feels he needs some extra fancy paintwork, so be it, for a captain boating carefully to protect his paintwork is also protecting the company's boat. What might seem somewhat wasteful and unnecessary from a financial point of view actually made good economic sense. If your boatman wanted to do it himself, to add decorations of his own, well, that too was obviously to be encouraged. The more personal involvement that the crew have with their boat, the more they will look after it.

Amongst the owner-boatmen the incentive was to save money, to paint the boat oneself to save the expense of having to employ someone else to do it, mowing the lawn to avoid paying a gardener. Both ideas spring from the conviction that these jobs have to be done anyway, which is not actually true. The garden can become a wilderness of nettles without affecting life in the house, and boats do not need painted flowers to perform their transport function. But conditioning, the expectations of the neighbours, the common politeness of not creating eyesores demands action from most people who are not totally insensitive to the feelings of others. So weekends are spent weeding and pruning, although planting elaborate flower beds in the front garden, like painting masses of diamonds and roses on boats, is far beyond social courtesy. Maintenance becomes a personal pleasure, a hobby, and the delightful result gives a much deeper satisfaction to both owner and onlooker.

Possibly the biggest boost to the emergence of the boatman-painter as an important part of the history of boat painting came from those who most wished to end it. The Grand Union Canal Company was formed in 1929 to promote an integrated canal network between London, Birmingham and Leicester, and they soon extended their routes into Nottinghamshire as well. They bought boats to provide a carrying service on their waterways, and by 1934 the Grand Union Canal Carrying Company operated twelve pairs of narrow boats. Decisions were then taken to expand the fleet even more dramatically and optimistically; massive orders were placed at Rickmansworth, Northwich and Woolwich that built up the fleet to nearly 400 craft within three years. It was a bold attempt to pull canal carrying into the twentieth century, but the clean-cut modern image that they set out to promote certainly did not include any traditional decorations.

The colour scheme was an austere two tones of blue with white lines between them, and hearts, scalloped edges and ogee arches on the cabin backs were replaced with rectangular simplifications. Roses and castles were not to be seen. It was after all the 1930s, an age of streamlining and simplicity, still reacting and recovering from the frills and excesses of Victorian and Edwardian taste, and it would not be surprising if the new management saw the old-fashioned paintings and colours as symptomatic of the inefficient attitudes that they had to overcome if they were to compete with aeroplanes and the motor lorry. The colour scheme changed to a more cheerful red, white and blue in Coronation year 1937,

but wartime austerity again provided ample reason to simplify the outside paint-work, and the company name was even reduced to simple initials. For well over a decade this was the company policy of the only large narrow boat carrying concern with a positive expansionist outlook as they set about finding new traffic.

It was a bold plan, but it never quite came to fruition. New traffic did not materialise quite quickly enough, and they started to compete with the established coal carriers to the detriment of both. There was a long established convention among canal carriers not to poach boat crews directly from each other, and the Grand Union Company, even if they nudged that policy a little, could never find quite enough good crews to put all their new boats into commission. Perhaps if they had not been so intransigent in their attitude to fancy paintwork, they would have been more successful in attracting boatmen to their big new boats. However, the cultural vacuum that they created with that policy certainly seems to have encouraged the emergence of the boatman-painter as a class on those southern routes. If the company wouldn't do it for them, they would do it for themselves.

When the canals were nationalised in 1948 it was those same Grand Union boats which formed the bulk of the narrow boat carrying fleet, although they were soon to be hugely augmented by the Fellows, Morton & Clayton fleet. The new management, largely the old team under a new name, also produced a new

*R*eg Barnett (right) paints a *water can, while Joe Tyler touches up the diamonds on one of his gangplank struts, watched by an appreciative audience of boat children. Their boats were all tied up at Bull's Bridge depot when this photograph was taken in the long cold winter of 1962–63, the one that caused the ending of canal carrying by the nationalised fleet.*

utilitarian colour scheme and once more pursued a simplification policy towards the paintwork. But times and attitudes were changing and a heated public debate took place which will be more fully discussed in Chapter 7. Despite the discussions, little really changed along the towpath, and it still remained largely up to the boatmen-painters to keep their cans and cabins decorated.

For some of the most talented boatman-painters there was a direct financial incentive too, which further undermines the 'amateur' label discussed earlier. Boating has never been well paid, and any part-time occupation which could earn some extra money was very welcome, especially as the itinerant nature of their job made it difficult to find any regular extra work on the bank. Painting cans and handbowls for friends and workmates could earn some extra income, whether paid for in cash or kind, for there was always some trading to be done with goods from damaged cases at the docks or the warehouse. These were the perks of the trade – although it might be better not to ask how some of the cases got damaged in the first place!

Increasingly however, the main market since World War II has been the pleasure boat business, either directly with the owners of converted boats or new cruisers, or indirectly through the canalside shops that steadily increased in numbers as the holiday trade developed. All needed small souvenirs to sell, and some acted as factors of the bigger traditional items to a more discerning clientele. This was a perfect channel for some of the boatmen, for they could paint up a number of items whilst tied up at either end of their trips and sell them to the shops as they travelled through. Shops at Stoke Bruerne and Long Buckby in the 1960s did a great deal to encourage some of the remaining Grand Union boat people to develop their hobby into a useful trade. As carrying finished, so holiday boating burgeoned. Many of those who painted whilst on the boats found new outlets for their art when they moved into houses and had more space, or retired and had more time. Happily, some ex-boating painters are still at work, and still producing paintwork that expresses something of that special relationship between boat art and their working life.

Paintwork by boatmen varies wildly, from excellent to horrible, and in a great variety of styles. To an even greater degree than the professionals, they are painting to a formula learned or copied from an existing style of boat painting. There has been little reference to nature, or to the way that fine art has portrayed nature, only to what has always been acceptable in the canal world as canal boat art. This sounds like a negative criticism but it is not, because the boatman-artist's talent and natural sense of design are then concentrated on repeating and improving that formula, and the results can be a purer and more personal piece of abstract design. Few canal boat flowers look like flowers anyway, when viewed with a cold dispassionate eye. They have a floral effect – they are colourful and arranged in bouquets or garlands, but it is the juxtaposition of blobs of colour with a green leaf pattern that cues the eye to read them as flowers far more than as an accurate depiction of petals, stamens and stem. They are simply items in the process of pattern making and decorating, with no real intention of re-creating an image of nature, but they are not the less important for that.

What is often apparent in the work of the boatman-painter is a difference of attitude. It may be more clumsily done, but there is a calm confidence that the art belongs to him and to his extended family working on the boats. There is less hurry to get the job finished (and paid for) and more care was taken to satisfy the

Ex-boatman Ike Argent and an example of his beautiful paintwork on a water can he painted in 1992. He says his style of rose is a personal development of the flowers that he was most familiar with in his youth, the roses of the Rudkin Bros dock at Leicester.

(Above)

The back door of a tunnel headlamp painted with a lively bunch of canal flowers by an unknown painter, discovered in a derelict state at Thos. Clayton's yard at Oldbury in 1964. The simplicity suggests that it was probably painted by a boatman, but one with a very strong sense of design and considerable skill.

◆◆

A range of items in the Boat Museum collection decorated by Harry Bentley in his own gentle version of the Hodgson style. Harry and his wife were both from Cheshire boating families. They worked for the Anderton Company when they were first married, where they got to know Bill Hodgson and his work very well.

demands of his well informed customers who were, before the pleasure boat business took over, judging what was right or acceptable in the boating world on the basis of a lifetime's experience, or on that of their parents and grandparents. Commercialism, producing work for sale to anybody who has the money to spend, does tend to undermine that personal relationship, but values instilled almost from birth within the tight community have usually withstood temptation pretty well. The work of many boatmen-painters is still a good yardstick against which to judge the mass productions of modern souvenir painters or the efforts of hobby painters who have hijacked the canal tradition into house and garden ornaments. There is still an honesty and an historic continuity.

Traditional boat painting also provided the means to satisfy an important

◆◆

Boatman Alan Brookes poses with a water can aboard his pair of Grand Union Canal Carrying Co boats.

psychological need for some as boatmen moved from boat to bank, a bridge from one lifestyle to another. As canal traffic diminished, the crews were forced to move off the boats; moving into a house on the bank was always an upheaval, but for some ex-boaters who had never lived ashore it must have been traumatic. All the conventions of house dwelling had to be learned; for the men under retirement age a new job had to be found. Generally the women adjusted more quickly, for a woman's traditional work was much easier in a house with running water and electricity than on a boat, and the children were easier to keep clean and get educated; but some of their menfolk found it more difficult. Whatever the new job, it was almost certainly a less individualistic and independent one than being a canal boat captain. True, the working hours were probably shorter and the wages better, but those benefits had to be set against their loss of authority, for their emasculation as tradesmen as a lifetime's skill was set aside, and deemed redundant. It became a familiar pattern throughout British industry in the 1970s and 1980s, but in the 1950s and 1960s it was still unusual, and unrecognised as a problem. However, there were jobs to go to, which was a help, and the transition was made, although often with considerable regret. Roses and castles were sometimes a help, a respected hobby and skill that brought their past life into the

present and helped re-adjustment, especially if it could earn some extra money.

As respect for the boat population has increased on the back of nostalgia, so the self respect of the boatmen and their descendants has also taken a proud turn. Where just a few years ago people were reticent to admit that they were of boating stock, relatives of 'water gypsies', now they are proud to declare their ancestry, proud that they are descendants of the clean hard-working tradesmen of the canals, with all their traditions and skills. Those include the painting tradition of course, and it is encouraging to discover the sons and grandsons of ex-boat people, for whom regular canal carrying is no more than a distant memory or even just a family tale, taking up the craft and continuing in some cases the family style. Because it is a hobby without the need to count every minute painting at a paid rate, some thoughtful canal painting keeps creeping into existence.

The work of a few of these boatmen-artists is shown in the accompanying illustrations, but the reader is once more asked to remember that those mentioned by name are only a tiny proportion of the boat people who could or did do it for themselves. For most of them the time and opportunity for painting was very limited, and their output was small. The results, from a less practised hand were also often crude, however much love and respect was invested in their production, and a lot of this clumsy art had a very short life.

This author's conclusion at present is that there was a large amount produced, but the greater professional output from the relatively few dockyard painters, added to the superficial attractiveness of their slick brushwork means that a much greater proportion of their work survives. This leaves an unresolved picture of the situation in the heyday of narrow boat carrying, and the relative proportions of amateur to professional work will always have to be conjecture.

Alan Barnett of Middlewich with some recently completed work in his garden workshop in January 1994, painted in his 'knobstick' style that he learned from his father Ralph.

CHAPTER 6

THE UNCONVENTIONAL
TRADITION

A 1937 hand bowl by Bill Hodgson carrying the boatman's favourite non-castle image, the 'sailor's head' of the Player's cigarette company trade mark.

A table-cupboard painted with a horse's head by Ike Argent, but with flowers added by 'Young' Charlie Atkins, who was a very prolific boatman-painter and collector, and whose grandson now continues the family painting tradition in Banbury.

For some professional tradesmen the job of boat painting overflowed into their private lives outside working hours. It became a hobby as well as a job, and sometimes an obsession. Once released, the skills developed for decorating boats seemed to need further channels for expression, and the standard boat tradition became a gateway or catalyst to something more private, a personal need to create. The satisfaction of being able to use the boat painting formula successfully helped to release any inhibitions about art generally, and it gave some of these unsophisticated artists the courage to experiment far more widely. The results range from delightful naïve to extreme kitsch, from touching innocence to heavy-handed attempts at academic art.

At one end of the scale is the self-conscious art of Bill Hodgson, clearly a Victorian decorator caught out in the twentieth century. He painted scenery and pictures before he painted boats, pastoral landscapes with cottages and ruins, and moments of stage drama, but having found a job and acceptance on the canal, his ambitions as an artist-decorator were largely channelled through the traditional ingredients of roses and castles. But they became much more than a way of earning extra money in the evening, they were what he did and what he was; his art defined his character.

J. Harry Taylor in Chester was another boat decorator who had some scenery painting experience when he was a young man. Any aspirations he might have harboured in that direction, however, were cut short when he inherited his father's boatyard in Walsall in 1889. For unknown reasons he eventually moved

Signwriting and decoration by J. Harry Taylor at Chester in the early 1920s. He is reported to have used a picture of the Water Tower at Chester as his pattern and trade mark, just across the basin from his original Chester boatyard, but this example seems to be an imaginary landscape.

this business to the Shropshire Union Canal, to Gobowen in 1909 and finally to Chester in 1911. When the SUC Company decided to stop carrying in their own boats in 1921 Taylor's took over their dockyard at Tower Wharf where they continued to maintain the boats of the bye-traders who took over some of the Shropshire Union carrying work. Harry Taylor did the necessary decorating work for the firm, using the usual canal convention, but he also continued to paint pictures as a pastime quite separately to his profession. As the proprietor of a large boatyard business he was a member of local middle class society, and his surviving paintings reflect that social position. There are polite landscapes of course, but also a series of stern family portraits suitable for an Edwardian parlour wall. Both Harry Taylor and Bill Hodgson were obviously aware of the respectable academic art standards of their time, and were artistically educated in a way that most other canal boat painters were not.

In the middle of the range are those painters who were clearly proud of their abilities, who were happy to do in the evening for friends and family what they did in the daytime for a job, but who satisfied their artistic needs with the basic traditional ingredients, within the constraints of the boat painting conventions. Frank Nurser and Isaiah Atkins would both fit this category. Their innate artistic abilities emerge through the constant repetition and re-arrangement of the set imagery; because they each had a strong personal sense of design and balance, conventional decoration done by them became a very individual personal art. Both occasionally used other imagery in their canal painting but not often enough for us to interpret the variations as any sort of cry for individuality. Frank painted a fine cockerel on a cabin block for one of Charles Nelson's boats, but this was their trade mark, and poultry was Frank Nurser's main occupation away from the dock, so it is not quite so unusual as it might seem at first glance. He occasionally painted a dog's head on a hand bowl bottom by way of a change, but not nearly so often as Bill Hodgson produced dogs, horses and sailor's heads. Isaiah Atkins occasionally replaced his castle picture on a boat stool with a painting of Polesworth church, or of Little Jim's Cottage, a local picturesque black and white thatched cottage which he copied from a postcard, but in general he was satisfied with his own fantasy castles learned at the dock.

Frank Jones developed a recognisable style and standard that would have satisfied most men in the trade, but he clearly felt a need to take it another stage further. His reputation as a boat artist encouraged him into more adventurous experiments at home where he painted a variety of non-boat related objects with a variety of designs; flowers on firescreens, crinoline ladies on mirrors, and a startling pair of trays with portraits of Montgomery and Eisenhower. They are impressive, but lack that subtle rightness of the relationship between the conventional canal boat art and its job on the water as part of boat life.

Most boat painters used some imagery that was not strictly 'roses and castles' at some time, and it is perhaps a measure of the vitality of the tradition that it was able to accommodate some fresh ideas quite late in its development. In 1875 a Birmingham newspaper reporter visited a narrow boat and noted 'a gay pictorial pail . . . enriched by designs of outrageous roses and sunflowers, while the bottom offers a good ground where upon to depict a gay cavalier or valiant crusader in full armour'. A very old panel of boat painting in Abingdon shows just such an image, a mounted soldier in red coat, plumes and breeches galloping bravely out of the past towards us. A stag leaping a hedge is reported to have

been a painted trademark of the Rudkin Bros. dock in Leicester, perhaps a boat painter's version of one of Sir Edwin Landseer's immensely famous and popular pictures, just as Landseer's many dewy-eyed sentimental pictures of Queen Victoria's dogs changed the idea of dog portraiture into a perennial popular art favourite.

Oddest of the oddities is the adoption by the canal painters of the 'Hero' sailor's head trademark of Player's Navy Cut cigarettes as a purely decorative picture. Famous paintings becoming trademarks are more common ('Bubbles' by Sir John Millais as used by Pears soap was one of the first examples, and is still perhaps the most famous), but a trademark becoming art is very rare. This 'Hero' of the cigarette packet gradually developed from various versions in the late nineteenth century, and the complete unit of portrait, lifebelt, and two ships was finally registered in 1891. The sailor's head with HMS *Britannia* on the left and the battleship HMS *Dreadnought* on the right became a very popular image with the boat people, and it was painted on cabin blocks and cupboard doors as well as its most common situation on the bottom of a hand bowl, where the design neatly fits the shape of the tinware. Its popularity is patriotic, for it was widely but quite wrongly believed to be a portrait of King George V, the 'sailor king' who had served in the navy from 1879 until 1892. Very early versions of this advertisement to show a bearded officer with lots of gold braid, and perhaps the popular connection with royalty started then. One particularly fine example by Bill Hodgson is dated 1937 and it may be significant that this was a very royalty conscious period that included the Jubilee of 1935, and the abdication crisis and subsequent coronation of King George VI in 1937.

As an island race the British have often regarded the sea and ships as a generally patriotic image – Britannia ruling the waves with the wooden walls of old England, and pictures of ships appear on several old water cans, but as the twentieth century progressed pictures of steamships and famous liners became tinged with patriotism too, symbols of the supremacy of British industry and the Empire. Pictures of the *Queen Mary* and similar ships are recorded several times in the canal boat tradition, but the decoration of the *Gerda* described in T. W. Cubbon's 1928 book *Only a Little Cock Boat* must surely have been, if true, the final frontier, '. . . the panels of the cabin being filled with fanciful pictures of hardy Norsemen sailing among floes, all gorgeous with a setting of Aurora Borealis'. Or was this an author in full poetic flow describing a viking ship sailing in the usual canal boat lake, mountains and sunset? That sort of popular image would not be surprising, whereas the inclusion of human figures certainly would be.

Most boat artists recognised their own limitations when approaching the truly naturalistic art of portraiture, where a minor mishandling of scale or detail so easily leads to grotesquerie. Everybody is so practised at reading the subtleties of body language and facial expression that it needs a considerable artistic knack and much practice to create an image of a human being that is comfortable to live with. There are no expectations as to what exact colour or size the castle or

The trade mark of the John Player's cigarette company, the 'sailor's head' of the canal boat tradition. This version is from a magazine of 1900.

The wartime heroes Ike and Monty commemorated on a pair of trays painted by Frank Jones soon after World War II, an unusual departure into portraiture for a canal painter.

mountains should be in an imaginary landscape, but the tiniest errors in a portrait can immediately create a cross-eyed dwarf.

George Baxter was clearly one of the painters who wanted to bend the rules. He learned his trade in the 1920s at the 'Limited' dock, the boatyard operated by the Samuel Barlow Coal Company (Ltd.) at Amington, near Tamworth, and learned his painting from the foreman, Len Shakespeare. Len, according to his apprentice, was an extremely good painter but one who refused to expand his pictorial palette beyond the standard necessities, and in his case the castle pictures always consisted of very similar paintings of a church with a spire. George remembers very little variation from one decorative panel to the other, or from one boat to the next, an artistic situation that did not satisfy this young boatbuilder and keen painter, who consequently tried to make every one of his panels a separate artistic composition.

In the 1930s he had two separate periods of employment at Walker's dock at Rickmansworth, and although initially employed as a straightforward boatbuilder, W. H. Walker soon recognised his potential as a decorator and sign-writer and employed him in that capacity as the need arose. The main customer at that point, however, was the Grand Union Canal Carrying Co. whose policy for paintwork was severe in the extreme. Opportunities for any extravagant boat decoration were limited to the boats of the smaller companies, to items painted for the boatmen themselves as 'foreigners' outside of company hours, and to a few panels inside the cabins.

On one of these panels, the biggest one over the side-bed, George decided, against all the usual conventions, to paint a large picture of a Red Indian in full war paint and feathers. He worked from the memory of a picture he had had at home as a child, and worked on it a bit at a time during the week that the boat was on dock. It certainly created a sensation, because the boatman hated it and complained to Mr Walker, and Walker had to ask George not to do this sort of thing again. Apparently the family were frightened of this stern warrior staring fiercely off the wall of their tiny cabin, and as we can be sure that George, like every other untrained artist, would have worked very hard on the eyes to make them 'follow you round the room', the response is perhaps understandable. Another of his painting experiments was to copy a picture advertising a local brewery, but he got told off for doing that too, and he learnt to keep his more imaginative ideas for boat decoration in check.

George returned to Samuel Barlow's for the duration of World War II, then did a short spell at the former Nurser dock at Braunston before returning to Glascote to work at S. E. Barlow's dock. There he remained until it closed in the 1960s, when his connection with boats and painting temporarily ceased.

In his retirement years he returned to painting as a hobby, but after a long period away from canal work, and freed from any commercial pressure or expectations, his painting became a much more personal art form. Despite sometimes including some recognisable boat painting ingredients, a bridge, trees, or a silhouetted castle in the distance, the atmosphere of these private pictures is

George Baxter, boatbuilder and boat painter at S. E. Barlow's dock at Tamworth, in retirement at home in 1993 with a recently completed cabin stool.

A painting by George Baxter, one of several simple pictures painted as a pastime during his retirement. Certain boat painting commercial techniques are still apparent, but the mysterious atmospheric landscape is now of greater importance and interest than the castle building, and has become a far more personal artistic statement.

◆◆

(Below)
Cabin side of the Rodney photographed at the first IWA Festival of Boats and Arts at Market Harborough in 1950. Decoration by George Baxter, then working at S. E. Barlow's dock at Anchor Bridge, Glascote.

◆◆

quite different to the professional sleight of hand of the practising boat painter. His years in the trade merely provided a gateway for his own imaginative landscapes to develop into far more individual statements. Years of practice still gives him control of his materials, but he remains unsophisticated in his attitude to art. A combination of his imagination and a natural sense of design has created a striking and delightful series of works of fresh naïve art.

CHAPTER 7

BLUE AND YELLOW, AND THE SOUVENIR DISEASE

When the canals were nationalised, the Grand Union Company's boats initially formed the bulk of the narrow boat carrying fleet. It was shabby and run-down after a long period of wartime restrictions, and one of the new management's first instructions was an order to paint the boats in a new colour scheme – a fresh livery and corporate image for a new start. Although much of the management team remained unchanged, there was a determination to make a go of it, and a political will to bring in some reforms, both practical and social. With hindsight we can see that blanket policies about centralised planning and workers' rights were going to be very difficult to put into practice on the canal system. However good the theory, it was a difficult problem accommodating the traditional practices of a hard-working, largely illiterate population of canal workers, used to exercising considerable freedom of action as captains of their own boats within any national policy. It was a challenge, but the problems were dramatically increased when Fellows, Morton & Clayton decided to cease trading, and offered their fleet of boats and their accompanying crews for nationalisation in November 1948. This made canal transport planning far more viable

Tom Ditton signwriting the Grand Union Canal Carrying Company's wartime utility initials on a butty at the Bull's Bridge depot.

The painter's workshop at Bull's Bridge in the early days of nationalisation, with a thoroughly decorated headlamp on the table, and plenty of cans and hand bowls awaiting attention.

and more countrywide, but it doubled the number of boats to bring up to standard, and doubled the population of boat crews under their direct jurisdiction.

The Docks & Inland Waterways Executive (DIWE) did try however, and a new simple colour scheme in yellow and blue was the visual public statement to that effect, the image of a modern, efficient, centralised industry. The boat population did not think much of it, but their voice was no more likely to be heard in the higher levels of management then, never mind listened to, than it had been in Grand Union days; but public opinion was stirring too. The publication of *Narrow Boat* by Tom Rolt, and the emergence of the fledgling Inland Waterway Association (IWA) had changed public awareness of canals in some significant quarters, and an increasing number of influential people now saw the hard-pressed population of the narrow boats as symbolic of a whole set of old-fashioned standards which were in danger of being bulldozed out of existence by the drive for efficiency and social planning. Far from being seen as an encumbrance on productivity, these visionaries realised that interference with the traditions of the boat people was an attack on a number of valuable qualities that were important to a fully rounded working human life, a much broader view of efficiency than the bureaucratic mind could then envisage, never mind actually encourage. The 'Blue and Yellow' controversy was born.

The Labour government's Transport Act came into effect on 1 January 1948 and it was during that first year of nationalisation that the new colour scheme was announced. It was not until 1949 however that the decision really turned into a controversy, because the recommendations were by then becoming reality and the dreary results were visible. In a radio programme on 6 February Frank

Jones commented how strange it was to be painting his first boat for the DIWE in the new colours, plain blue and 'gold', with no decorations at all, and said the boatmen were already complaining about these dull looking boats. But the boating population's opinion was not likely to make much impact in the offices of the Executive; what they needed were champions from the middle classes, educated intellectuals who could fight the case where it mattered, in London, with access to the press. On 19 February Barbara Jones wrote a short impassioned letter to the editor of *The Times* defending the roses and castles of the narrow boats as the most vigorous of Britain's surviving vernacular arts, castigating the Executive for threatening to abolish them on utilitarian grounds, and defending them as part of the boat families' personal way of life. Barbara Jones was already a well-known designer and mural painter, an attractive woman with a lively personality, shortly to become even better known as an author and one of the key designers of the Festival of Britain. She was an early IWA supporter, lived in Highgate, and knew the sort of people who informed public opinion. Her own opinion was in turn greatly respected, and *The Times* followed her lead on that day, and included an editorial piece of their own in support of her case. They too thought that a policy of utilitarian uniformity was 'an over scrupulous economy . . . Flourishing traditional arts are not so plentiful nowadays that one of them can be wantonly sacrificed' it thundered. 'Let the Executive . . . remember that it will be a poor advertisement for national ownership should it insensitively destroy a well-loved flower that bloomed in the atmosphere of individualism.'

That was the stone that rippled the pond. Miss Jones received a massive postal response in support of her argument whilst most national newspapers followed *The Times* lead with critical articles of their own. *The Daily Express* carried a

Contrasting styles of paintwork on a pair of cabin stools, the first (left) painted with great professional verve and flair, possibly at the S. E. Barlow dock at Tamworth; the other (right) by boatman Tommy Lowe of Midddlewich, whose style is much more hesitant and naïve, but done with great care and affection. Between them, they exemplify the two ends of the tradition as it had developed by the 1960s.

Giles cartoon, and *The Times* carried another letter, this time from Peter Scott. He idealistically thought that 'the State should be the model employer, a trustee both for a unique tradition of beauty and for the general good appearance of the boats, an example to all other employers.' Margaret Lambert writing in the weekly periodical *Time and Tide* wanted government money to foster the survival of the popular arts, as was happening in other countries. 'Our Government, too, has lately been at pains to encourage traditional arts and crafts and even in these austere days has managed to find some money for this purpose. Where I suspect we are unique is in allowing one authority to muddle away the work of others by deliberately destroying what good money is being spent to preserve'. Once more the idealism of the hope for an integrated national arts policy in conjunction with transport is heart warming, but depressingly doomed with hindsight.

Complainants to the Executive by post received a standard letter that sought to deflect the criticism by reminding the reader that the DIWE only actually owned about one-sixth of the boats operating on the system, inferring that they thought the tradition was safe with the remaining privately-owned majority, regardless of what they themselves chose to do. Further protests were replied to with a weak statement that there were insufficient tradesmen to do the work anyway, which whilst being quite untrue, provided perfect ammunition for a counter argument in favour of apprenticeship schemes, providing fresh employment by the state owned industry as well as state support for some national folk art. The clamour for retention would seem to be overwhelming, but the determination of bureaucracy remained steadfast.

Much of the opposition was co-ordinated by the young IWA under the confrontational leadership of Robert Aickman. His autobiography *The River Runs Uphill* describes how the association was almost forced to embrace the controversy and support the argument, even though it seemed to some members, both then and since, to be very peripheral to the central concern of saving the waterways from further closure, or promoting traffic. Apart from the clear pressure of public opinion which it would have been foolish to ignore, the campaign was, he says, 'a marvellous propaganda opportunity for those with an eye and an instinct for such things', and he certainly had that instinct. But beyond those cold calculations of battle in the media war, he too was impassioned in the defence of roses and castles for themselves, for they 'were among the most beautiful and heart-warming things to be seen in the whole of Britain, and the last large scale and authentic survival of popular folk . . . They symbolised excellently the philosophy that the Association had been founded to uphold'.

The high spot of the campaign was probably the early evening broadcast on 2 July 1949 on the BBC Light Programme, of a discussion between two representatives from the Executive, and a powerful battery of people opposing the changes. Barbara Jones was there, Captain Patterson of the Samuel Barlow Coal Co represented the canal carriers, Sonia Smith spoke at length for the working boat population and Frank Nurser spoke for the painters. When tape recorded interviews from the boatmen were inserted too, even the BBC felt that the argument was getting too unbalanced, and Hal Jukes who chaired the programme introduced the final section by saying 'we're going to try and play fair by letting the Docks & Inland Waterways Executive have a two-to-one discussion with Mr Aickman . . .' No recording seems to exist of the ensuing debate, but knowing the forceful ability of Robert Aickman in argument one suspects that Mr Wilson

and Mr Goss of the Executive would have felt like terrier pups faced with an angry wolfhound by the end.

The public debate appeared to have been won by the conservationists, but it made very little difference in reality. Calls for this new state-owned industry to be an ideal model employer listening to public opinion and the demands of its own workers was hopelessly idealistic even then, as subsequent history has proved. But a few sops were handed down and the Executive's position officially softened, according to their public statements. The colour scheme was still only an 'experiment', the boats could keep their names instead of only being a number, only the dowdy former Grand Union Company boats would be affected, the traditional decorations of ex-Fellows, Morton & Clayton boats would be retained, although the boats would be repainted in the new livery. Eventually statements emerged that some roses and castles were to be re-introduced. The Executive's house magazine *Lock and Quay* reported in December 1949 that 'As these boats come in for overhaul [at Bull's Bridge depot] they are being repainted in the D&IWE house colours of blue and gold, and a decoration of roses and castles is being included, even on those boats which did not previously carry these traditional emblems'. Was this true? Had the argument been won?

Considering that it is such recent history, it is surprisingly difficult to disentangle what actually happened from what was supposed to happen. There were two complicating influences, the first from the dock painters, the second from

Mrs Lapworth with the youngest member of the crew of British Waterways butty Cheam *in front of a well decorated pair of cabin doors, possibly from Freeman's dock, Dudley.*

Lock & Quay

D & I W E

DECEMBER, 1949
Price 3d.

DOCKS AND INLAND WATERWAYS EXECUTIVE

*T*he first colour scheme for the newly nationalised narrow boats had the main side panels yellow, with a blue border, but this was subsequently reversed. On the D&IWE magazine cover at the end of the second year of their existence freshly painted roses and castles from the Bull's Bridge workshop are clearly visible, but this original and individual work was soon to be replaced by transfers.

the boatmen. In the initial confusion of reorganisation, and whilst the idealism of the new management's policy was still fresh, boats were docked and repainted at many smaller boatyards as well as at the main depot at Bull's Bridge. Repainting was certainly carried out at the private docks at Braunston, Rickmansworth, and Leighton Buzzard, and the two FM&C dockyards at Saltley and Uxbridge soon became part of the equation, too. At all these yards the painters were interpreting the Executive's colour directives in their own way, and photographic evidence shows a surprising variety of treatments of the basic yellow and blue, considering that it was supposed to be a unifying company livery. Some were outlined with thin lines, others had broad stripes or swooping curves; some clearly had roses and castles on the doors whilst others did not. Things were rationalised somewhat when the Uxbridge yard was closed down and men were transferred to Bull's Bridge, which then became and remained the main depot and maintenance yard for the Southern narrow boat fleet. Painters Tom Ditton and Jack Phillips at Southall were joined by Harry Crook and Henry Penn from Uxbridge, and there was plenty of painting talent and experience available to decorate the boats if the management would sanction it.

Nearly twenty years of the Grand Union's policy of not officially decorating their boats had, however, left another legacy, a group of boatmen who were already accustomed to decorating their own boats, painting roses and pictures on the doors, and inside the cabins. The GUCC Co., whilst refusing to pay for any decoration beyond basic cabin graining had been quite happy to let the boatmen do their own fancy work, and a lot of capable painters had developed their skill, and something of a proud tradition of doing it themselves. This too continued into the nationalised fleet, and photographs of well decorated Grand Union Company boats or early British Waterways boats are just as likely to feature the work of a boatman-painter as that of one of the professional dockyard painters.

The standard castle picture that was applied by transfer to the nationalised narrow boat fleet in an attempt to appease the boat population's demand for decoration whilst cutting the cost of craftsmanship.

And then some dull bureaucratic mind thought of transfers. Here at last it seemed was a cheap and boring way out of the ideological mess they had found themselves in when they inherited a lively popular art tradition which their accountants could not understand. Cheap transfers applied to all the cabin doors would appease the ignorant boat population's need for some art, without involving the management in any of the costs of continuing craftsmanship, individuality or originality. What a depressingly sad comment on the time, and on the management's attitude, a patronising poverty of imagination.

In fact these transfers were quite successful and surprisingly popular, not least because they were based on a design by Frank Jones from Leighton Buzzard. The printing techniques of the time, the simplified way the colours were separated out for screen printing, gives a rather harsh comic book quality to the pictures which sacrifices all subtlety of blending or colour, but the bunches of roses were more successful. They were cheap of course, compared to the time taken by a painter or signwriter (for most of the lettering was applied by transfer as well) but they were all the same, ad infinitum, and a far cry from the delights of the individual paintings on Barlow's boats for example, or the richness of Bill Hodgson's paintwork on the Trent & Mersey. It could be argued that they were a step in the right direction, away from a complete absence of anything, but they were also a step toward an acceptance of uniformity and a lack of individuality. Time ran out, however, before any real long term effect could be judged, because the hard winter of 1962–63 provided just the reason that the management had been looking for to wind up the carrying fleet, and to rid themselves of the responsibility of their itinerant boat population and their awkward culture. For the last few years of family boat carrying, it was the Willow Wren fleet and the Samuel Barlow boats, now under the ownership of Blue Line Cruisers, that carried the banner and burden of maintaining the tradition towards the present. Regular traffic finished in 1970, and it is now just a few individual boat owners who carry occasional loads of domestic fuel that keeps alive the concept of canal carrying by narrow boat.

As regular carrying by narrow boat was dying away, the holiday business was booming. Increasing numbers of hire boats and private pleasure boats replaced the real thing with replicas, both in artifacts and attitudes, and the boat painting tradition suffered a steep decline. A new breed of souvenir painters gave a glance at some original work, noticed that it was relatively simple and therefore decided it must be easy as well. However, that simplicity is subtle and deceptive, and without careful consideration it is easy to use the concept of folk art as an excuse to market deliberate attempts at contrived clumsiness. Most corrupting of all is the self-deception of some of this new breed of painter who convince themselves that, although they are people from different backgrounds producing work for a different class of customer for an entirely different purpose, they are nevertheless a natural part of the folk art of the canals. From there they proceed to promote their work, regardless of quality or continuity of style, as something that is helping to preserve the tradition when in fact it is smothering it to death. Those of us in the business need to tread very carefully and respectfully if we are not to destroy that which we desperately want to preserve.

From what seemed to be a terminal decline in the 1970s the boat painter's art seems to be recovering and staggering into a new age, although the numerous canal shops still sell very junky souvenirs painted with the fewest possible flowers

Close-up of the cabin side castle on Angela, *featured opposite.*

at the greatest possible speed by people with little understanding of the real thing. This is a great pity because the holiday making customers are by their nature probably new to the subject, trustingly spending their money on what is presented to them as canal art, and hoping they are helping to keep that art alive. They cannot be expected to deploy an accurate critical judgement so early in their canal experience, so it must be the duty of the painters and the shop keepers to understand the difference and to maintain standards. Amongst boat owners, however there has been a resurgence of interest in good quality painting, and the future looks more secure.

There is, for example, a dedicated band of enthusiasts who maintain and restore ex-working boats to a high standard, but good quality work is also being commissioned by the owners of modern canal cruisers whose new boats now cost so much that money spent on a good professional painting job will still only be a tiny proportion of the whole. Most have had a boat on the canal before and are already familiar with the tradition, and some have a very exacting standard of decoration in mind. It is the icing on their cake, the hap'orth of tar without which the ship would be spoiled, and a new order of professional boat painter is emerging to satisfy that market. With respect for the work of the past and a careful and responsible attitude to their own work, now these modern craftsmen and women can carry the canal tradition forward into the twenty first century quite satisfactorily. It will be an art artificially preserved, but it will still be valuable evidence about a possible and positive human relationship between sensible transport, life, work and art on an everyday basis. This old-fashioned balanced relationship is going to become ever more desperately important in the future, and my hope is that this book can help to bring about a re-appraisal of these important values, so beautifully illustrated by the folk art of the canals.

George Baxter *putting the finishing touches to* Angela, *half a narrow boat converted to a hire cruiser at S. E. Barlow's dock in the 1950s.*

ACKNOWLEDGEMENTS

Flowers Afloat is to some extent a revision and extension of my first book *Narrow Boat Painting*, published by David & Charles in 1974. I would like to offer to all those people acknowledged in that book my continued thanks, for they all helped me to gather the basic information upon which my opinions and the present work is based. This book, however, attempts to give much more information and recognition to the individuals who were actually engaged in the business, and my first thanks must be due to the painters I have had the pleasure of meeting, and the families of those who have already stepped into history who have helped me to build a more personal picture of their lives and characters. Thank you Bob Allen, Isaiah Atkins, Frank Barr, George Baxter, Norah Beech, William Blunn, Marie Brassey, John Brooks, Catherine Bushell, Kaye Clarke, Thirza Clarke, George Crowshaw, Jack Hodgson, Ron Hough, Brenda and Lionel Jones, Olive Mills, Barbara Nurser, Maurice Nurser, Jess Owen, Doreen Parr, Alan Roberts, Geoff Taylor, Betty Thorpe, Herbert Tooley, and Fred Winnett.

One of the pleasures of working on the canals in any context is coming into contact with the working boat population, who have always tried to answer my questions with care and courtesy. I have received snippets of information from dozens of ex-boaters over the years, many of whose names I never knew anyway, but I am grateful to all of them. Some have been extremely helpful in my obsession with the paintwork and I would like to offer extra thanks to Bill Atkins, Ike Argent, William Baker, Alan Barnett, Alice and Reg Barnett, Sara and Harry Bentley, Horace Estcourt, Joe Harrison, Michael Whitlock and Frank Woodhouse.

In addition there are all the friends and acquaintances who have generously offered me information, access to their collections, accommodation, photographs, expertise, encouragement and inspiration over many years. Many thanks to Harry Arnold, Stephen Ballard, David Blagrove, Peter Borshik, Malcolm Braine, Malcolm Bristow, Canal Cruising Company at Stone, Tim Carter, Nigel Carter, Frank Cheshire, Brian Collings, Carol and Dennis Cooper, Graham Edgson, Lindy Foster, Peter Gould, Lynnette and Chris Griffiths, Leslie Hailes, Robin Hewitt, Boris Howarth, Andrew Jenkinson, Selwyn Jordan, Ken Keay, Peter Lead, Anne Luard, Bob May, Lynnette and Andy Millward, Alan Picken, John Pitman, John Pyper, Sonia Rolt, Diana Smith, Frank Southern, Wally Staines, Mike Sumner, Cath and Mike Turpin, Arthur Wood, Ian L. Wright and Edna Yates.

I have made much use of the specialist waterway museums, and my thanks are due to the staff and archivists at the Boat Museum at Ellesmere Port, The National Waterways Museum at Gloucester Docks and the Canal Museum at Stoke Bruerne; several other museums have also been generous and helpful with access and information, and have allowed me to see and photograph items in their reserve collections. I would like to acknowledge the help given by Abingdon Park Museum at Northampton, Birmingham Science Museum, Blakes Lock Museum in Reading, Gloucestershire Folk Museum, Rural History Centre in the University of Reading, Snibstone Discovery Park (Leicestershire Museums) and the Wedgwood Museum at Barlaston.

The monthly magazine *Waterways World* has consistently encouraged my research, and has published a number of short articles by me about canal boat painting, which has led to much interesting correspondence and information. I would like to thank the magazine's publisher for commissioning these articles, some parts of which are now included within the text of this book.

I have been constantly indebted to two outstanding canal historians: to Alan Faulkner, the author of *The Grand Junction Canal* (1993) and a host of thoroughly researched articles about individual canal carrying companies which have been published in *Waterways World* and in booklet form by Robert Wilson; and to Edward Paget-Tomlinson, the author of *The Illustrated History of Canal and River Navigations* (1993) and the artist-researcher of the encyclopaedic series 'Colours of the Cut' also published in the *Waterways World* magazine.

Finally, thanks to my wife Mary once more for her unwavering support and encouragement throughout the research and writing of this book, and for disentangling and transforming my appalling handwritten manuscript into another neat clear typescript.

ILLUSTRATION ACKNOWLEDGEMENTS

Photographs and drawings are reproduced with the kind permission of the following individuals and organisations:

Harry Arnold 21, 50, colour pictures 6, 20, 42; Stephen Ballard colour picture 9; Alice Barnett 62; Boat Museum Archive, Ellesmere Port 1 (Ware coll.) 8, 9, 10, (K. C. Ward), 15 (Ware coll.), 40 (Mrs Temple Thurston), 42 (Ware coll.), J; Marie Brassey 46; British Waterways Archive, Gloucester 7, 38, 51, 69, 70, 71; John Brooks 37; Canal Cruising Co. Stone 74, (original photograph by Fred Armstong); Tim Carter 72; Cheshire Record Office 59; Coventry Evening Telegraph 28; A. Deakin 57; Alan Faulkner 2, 33; Eily Gayford collection 12, 22, 23, 29; Jack Hodgson 47; Jim Hollinshead 43; Ron Hough 34; Illustrated London News Library 11; Lionel Jones colour picture 31; Selwyn Jordan 61; Liverpool Museum 3; Manchester Public Library 48; Bob May 5; National Gallery 16; National Geographic Magazine 52; National Waterways Museum 4; Barbara Nurser 6, colour picture 15; Maurice Nurser 31; E. W. Paget Tomlinson/Geoff Taylor 65; Rural History Centre, Reading 55, 63; Tamworth Castle Museum 73; Betty Thorpe 39, 41, G; Executors of D. J. Watkins Pitchford 49; Frank Woodhouse 20; Ian L. Wright 30, 67.

All other photographs are by the author or are from prints in the author's collection.

BIBLIOGRAPHY

Aickman, Robert *The River Runs Uphill* (J. M Pearson, Burton on Trent, 1986)

Ayres, James *British Folk Art* (Barrie and Jenkins, London, 1977)

Ayres, James *English Naive Painting* (Thames and Hudson, London, 1980)

Cubbon, T. W. *Only a Little Cock Boat* (George Roberts, London, 1928)

Faulkner, Alan *The George and the Mary* (Robert Wilson, Kettering, 1973)

Faulkner, Alan *The Grand Junction Canal* (W. H. Walker and Brothers Ltd, Rickmansworth, 1993)

Hanson, Harry *The Canal Boatmen 1760–1914* (Manchester University Press, Manchester, 1975)

Hassel, John *A Tour of the Grand Junction Canal in 1819* (Reprinted Cranfield and Bonfield Books, London, 1968)

Hollingshead, John *On the Canal* (Originally published in *Household Words* magazine 1858. Reprinted Waterway Museum, Stoke Bruerne, 1973)

Jones, Barbara *The Unsophisticated Arts* (The Architectural Press, London, 1951)

Jones, Yvonne *Georgian and Victorian Japanned Ware of the West Midlands* (Museum catalogue) (Wolverhampton Art Gallery and Museums, Wolverhampton, 1982)

Lead, Peter *The Trent and Mersey Canal* (Moorland Publishing, Ashbourne, 1980)

Loomes, Brian *White Dial Clocks* (David & Charles, Newton Abbot, 1981)

Lowndes, T. (ed) *The History of Inland Navigations* (London, 1779)

O'Connor, John, *Canals, Barges and People* (Art and Technics, London, 1950)

Paget-Tomlinson, Edward *The Illustrated History of Canal and River Navigations* (Sheffield Academic Press, Sheffield, 1993)

Robertson, H. R. *Life on the Upper Thames* (Originally published in *Art Journal* magazine 1873. Republished Virtue, Spalding and Co., London, 1875)

Rolt, L. T. C. *Narrow Boat* (Eyre and Spottiswoode, London, 1944)

Rolt, L. T. C. *The Inland Waterways of England* (George Allen and Unwin Ltd., London, 1950)

Smith, George *Our Canal Population* (Coalville, 1875)

Vale, Edmund *By Shank and Crank* (William Blackwood and Sons, Edinburgh and London, 1924)

Walker, Anthony *Walkers' of Ricky* (W. H. Walker and Brothers Ltd, Rickmansworth, 1991)

Wilson, Robert *Roses and Castles* (Waterways Museum, Stoke Bruerne, 1976)

MAGAZINES AND PERIODICALS

The Burlington Magazine Vol 49, 1926. Camilla Doyle, 'The Vanishing Arts of a Peasantry'

The Countryman Vol 39, Summer 1949. Frederick Burgess, 'Roses, Castles and Lozenges'

Lock and Quay House magazine of Docks and Inland Waterways Executive, September 1949 – December 1954. Many isolated references to paintwork, and to the Blue and Yellow house colours controversy.

Time and Tide A weekly journal which carried articles and correspondence about the Blue and Yellow colour scheme in March 1949.

The Times 19 February, 1949. Letter to the editor about the Blue and Yellow colour scheme, and editorial comment in support.

Visual Resources Vol 5, 1988. (Gordon and Breach, USA) Philip Pacey, 'The Poor Man's Claude Lorraines: Unravelling the Story of the Dissemination of an Image'

Waterways World Monthly magazine, published continuously to the present since 1972, containing numerous articles and comments about painting, both historical and contemporary.

FILM

Painted Boats Ealing Studios, 1945

RADIO PROGRAMMES

Country Magazine BBC Home Service, 6 February, 1949. Painter Frank Jones in conversation with Ralph Wightman and others.

Kaleidoscope 'Canal Culture' BBC Radio 4, 26 September, 1992. Chris Eldon-Lee explores the narrow boat traditions.

Roses and Castles BBC Light Programme, 24 June, 1949. A discussion programme including contributions from Robert Aickman, Barbara Jones, Sonia Smith and others.

William Hodgson BBC Radio Stoke, 1983. Arthur Wood researches the life and work of Bill Hodgson, boat painter of Stoke on Trent.

INDEX